EDWARD MILLER

His Life and Times

EDWARD MILLER
Painted and engraved by Thomas Hardy.

EDWARD MILLER

Organist of Doncaster

His life and times

Written by

FREDERICK FOWLER

in collaboration with

J. EDWARD DAY

and

LESLIE SMITH

DONCASTER METROPOLITAN BOROUGH COUNCIL

EDUCATION SERVICES

This book is published jointly by the Museum and Arts Services
and the Libraries Service of Doncaster M.B.C.

Contributions towards the cost of publication have been received
from the Doncaster Arts and Museum Society, the Doncaster
Group of the Yorkshire Archaeological Society, the Friends of
Doncaster Parish Church and other patrons who wish to remain
anonymous.

The address of the publisher is Museum and Art Gallery,
Chequer Road, Doncaster, South Yorkshire. DN1 2AE

Printed by G. W. Belton Ltd., Gainsborough.

ISBN: 903524 13 9

'I stand ready with a pencil in one hand and a sponge in the other to add, alter, omit, enlarge and dilate according to better information. And, if these my pains shall be worthy to pass a second impression, my faults I will confess with shame, and amend with thankfulness, to such as will contribute clearer intelligence to me.'

THOS. FULLER
'History of the Worthies of England,' 1662.

ACKNOWLEDGMENTS

In our search for information it was both pleasing and encouraging to find that there were so many people who were only too willing to help. We acknowledge our indebtedness to the following:

Mr. John Barwick, Director of Museums and Arts Service, Doncaster; Mr. John Chapman, Chief Librarian, Doncaster; Mr. T. G. Manby, Curator, and Mr. M. J. Dolby, Keeper of Antiquities, Doncaster Museum; Mr. C. Howarth, Doncaster Reference Library; Mr. T. S. Alexander-Macquiban, Doncaster Borough Archivist, and Dr. D. Postles, City of Sheffield Archivist; the Rev. Canon G. Lawn, Vicar of St. George's Church, Doncaster, and Mr. Magnus Black, Master of the Music; Miss Joyce Wilkinson, Carr Grange, Doncaster; Mr. P. L. Scowcroft, Mr. P. Bear and Mr. G. Swann, Doncaster; Mr. Nicholas McGegan, London; Mrs. N. A. Bramwell, of Westerham, Kent; Mrs. M. E. Gleed, Secretary of the Royal Society of Musicians of Great Britain; Miss M. J. Kennedy, City and County Archivist, Norwich; Professor Nicholas Temperley and Mr. Carl Manns, of the University of Illinois School of Music; Dr. D. Hadley of the Dept. of History, Wake Forest University, North Carolina.

We offer grateful thanks also to the Directors/Librarians of the following institutions for assistance in our research:

The Music Library of the British Library, London; The Bodleian Library, Oxford; The University Library, Cambridge; The Rowe Music Library, King's College, Cambridge; The Guildhall Library, London; The Henry Watson Music Library, Manchester; The Borthwick Institute of Historical Research (University of York); and the Central Libraries of York, Leeds and Norwich.

For permission to use copyright and other material we thank:

The Metropolitan Borough of Doncaster; The Music Dept., Oxford University Press, ('The Oxford Companion to Music' and 'The Mirror of Music', both by Percy Scholes); The Macmillan Administration Basingstoke Ltd., ('Under the Greenwood Tree', Thomas Hardy); The Norfolk and Norwich Record Office, (The late Dr. A. H. Mann's manuscript on 'Norwich Musicians');* The Hogarth Press Ltd., ('The Development of English Biography', by Harold Nicolson, 1927); Geoffrey Bles, ('Charles Lindley, Viscount Halifax', by J. G. Lockhart, 1935-6, 2 Volumes).

---

* (Arthur Henry Mann, Mus. Doc., Organist, Teacher and Composer, was born in Norwich in 1850 and became a Cathedral Chorister there. From 1876 onwards he was Organist of King's College, Cambridge, where he died in 1929. We cannot over-emphasize the value to us of his manuscript mentioned above, more than twenty pages of which are devoted to Edward Miller).

ILLUSTRATIONS

Frontispiece - Edward Miller.

Chapter One

'Norwich is, as you please, either a city in an orchard, or an orchard in a city, so equally are houses and trees blended in it, so that the pleasure of the country and the populousness of the city meet here together.' Thus observed the seventeenth-century writer, Thomas Fuller, in his book, 'The Worthies of England'.The diarist Evelyn, after declaring Norwich to be one of the noblest cities in England, added further praise - 'The suburbs are large, the prospect sweete, and other amoenities, not omitting the flower gardens, which all the Inhabitans excell in.....' Daniel Defoe's account of his visit to the Norwich of 1723 - 'an antient, large, rich, and populous city' - is chiefly concerned with its trade and industry. He was impressed by the vast manufactures of the Norwich weavers and observed, that on weekdays, the streets appeared to be deserted - 'The inhabitants being all busie at their manufactures, dwell in their garrets at their looms, and in their combing-shops, so they call them, twisting-mills, and other work-houses; almost all the works they are employ'd in, being done within doors.' With the coming of the industrial revolution however, these textile trades gradually forsook Norwich and settled in distant areas of coal and steam, leaving the city with much of its beauty. Thus George Borrow, writing in 'Lavengro' towards the middle of the nineteenth century, was able to say - 'A fine old city.... view it from whatever side you will; but it shows best from the east, where the ground, bold and elevated, overlooks the fair and fertile valley in which it stands....Yes, there it spreads from the north to south, with its venerable houses, its numerous gardens, its thrice twelve churches, its mighty mound..... There is a grey old castle upon the top of that mighty mound; and yonder, rising three hundred feet above the soil, from among those noble forest trees, behold that old Norman masterwork, that cloud-encircled cathedral spire around which a garrulous army of rooks and choughs continually wheel their flight. Now, who can wonder that the children of that fine old city are proud of her, and offer prayers for her prosperity?'

It was in this 'fine old city', a decade or so after Defoe's visit, that Edward, the son of Thomas and Elizabeth Miller, was born. This occurred on October 30th 1735 in the parish of St. Peter Mancroft, and the registers of that church record his baptism on the 30th of November following. The father, Thomas, was a paviour, having served an apprenticeship to that trade, and at the time of Edward's birth, was a freeman of Norwich and also the City paviour. Thomas's brother, John, followed the same profession, the two having been apprentices together.

There was at least one other Miller living at that time who was concerned with paving, another Edward in fact, as we learn from the following notices. The 'Suffolk Mercury and St. Edmunds-Bury Post' informed its readers on September 6th 1725 that the White Hart Inn at Sudbury, 'being newly repaired and commodiously fitted up for the Reception of Gentlemen', was occupied by Edward Miller, Pavier, from Bury St. Edmunds. Nearly three years later, in the 'Norwich Gazette' of March 2nd 1728, Edward Miller, the Bury Pavier, advertised his boarding house near Bedlam, in Norwich, and on January 16th and 23rd 1742, the same paper told of Mr. Edward Miller's boarding house in St. Giles' Gate, adding that, 'he continues his paving as usual.' It is reasonable to assume that these three Edwards, all paviours and boarding house keepers, were one and the same person, but whether that person was a kinsman of brothers Thomas and John is not known.

Thomas and his wife Elizabeth had seven children all baptized in the church of St. Peter Mancroft. Their first-born, in 1729, was Elizabeth, followed by Thomas in 1731, Sarah 1733, Edward 1735, Mary 1740, Jane 1742-3 and Louise in 1746. Apart from their baptismal records nothing is definitely known of Elizabeth, Mary, Jane and Louise, but it is most likely that there were deaths in infancy. (See Appendix One).

The eldest son, Thomas, after serving his apprenticeship to a grocer, was able to start business on his own account at Bungay in Suffolk, at the early age of twenty-four. His fondness for reading led him to combine bookselling with his grocery, and to his stock of valuable books he also added engraved portraits. We learn from the 'Dictionary of National Biography' (p.423, Vol. 37) that he was interested in coins too, and in 1782 and 1790 he printed catalogues of his coin collections. He had one son, Wiliam Richard Beckford Miller, whom we shall meet later.

Of the paviour's second daughter Sarah, we know very little until she became the second wife of 'Doctor' William Norford, physician and man midwife. They were married on May 29th 1759 at Halesworth in Suffolk, where the doctor was in practice, but within a year or two they moved to Bury St. Edmunds. Sarah had ten children and was still living in 1804. There is a memorial tablet to her husband, who died in 1793, in the South Transept of St. Edmundsbury Cathedral.

Little is known of Edward's early years, but music must have featured prominently in his education. While still in his 'teens' he performed most proficiently on the German Flute, the name by which the fore-runner of the modern side-blown or transverse flute *(flauto traverso)* was generally known in this country, in order to distinguish it from the popular end-blown flute which we know today as the recorder.

The early transverse flutes were not provided with holes for the accidental notes, and when such notes were attempted, (by the method of cross-fingering) they were often out of tune or of poor quality. Towards the end of the seventeenth century an extra hole was bored for the lowest accidental (the one most difficult to play) and covered by a key. Miller's instrument would be of this type. In addition to being known as a German Flute it was also called a 'one-keyed flute' and, when performed today, is described as a Baroque Flute.

Though this addition was a great improvement it was not until the 1770's that three more holes with keys were added for other accidentals, opposition to this innovation coming from flautists themselves, who regarded the instrument as almost perfect and attributed any false intonation to lack of skill on the part of the player. Miller came to know this four-keyed flute (see pages 21 and 102), but it was not until more than thirty years after his death that the Boehm flute, with its greatly improved structure and mechanism was introduced to this country.

ST. PETER MANCROFT, NORWICH.
Lithograph by J. Sillett, published in 'Views of the churches, chapels and other public edifices in the City of Norwich, 1828'. (By courtesy, Norfolk County Library).

Chapter Two

Charles Burney was born in Shrewsbury on April 12th 1726 and attended the free school there. Later he moved to Chester, becoming a pupil of the free school in that city and studying music with Edmund Baker, the Cathedral organist. On returning to Shrewsbury, when about the age of fifteen, he continued to study music as a pupil of his half-brother James, who was organist at St. Mary's Church. In 1744 he was apprenticed to Thomas Augustine Arne and for three years lived with his elder brother Richard in London. We are told in Austin Dobson's 'Fanny Burney' (Macmillan, 1903) that he did not learn much from Arne except to copy music and to drudge in the Drury Lane orchestra which Arne conducted, but his charm and ability brought him many friends. He was frequently at the house of Arne's sister, Mrs. Cibber, the famous tragic actress, and there he made the acquaintance of many notabilities. Handel and Garrick were often among the visitors. In 1747, through an introduction made in the shop of Jacob Kirkman, harpsichord maker, Burney became acquainted with Fulke Greville, who paid Dr. Arne three hundred pounds to cancel the young musician's articles and took him into his own establishment. Not long afterwards, when Greville married, Burney gave away the bride, and later stood proxy for a duke at the baptism of Greville's first child. He should have travelled to Italy with the family in 1748 but was released from this contract when he wished to marry. In the next year he was appointed organist at St. Dionis Backchurch in Fenchurch Street which had been rebuilt by Wren after the Great Fire. He augmented his salary of thirty pounds a year by teaching and composing, but was later advised for health reasons to leave London, which he did in 1751, having secured the post of organist at St.Margaret's Church, King's Lynn, at an annual salary of one hundred pounds. He remained in Lynn for nine years during which time his health greatly improved. Travelling on horseback he gave lessons in many of the great houses of Norfolk, including Holkham, Houghton, Felbrigg and Rainham. On returning to the capital in 1760 he was much in demand as a teacher to society families. The degrees of Bachelor and Doctor of Music were conferred on him by Oxford University, and in 1770, he visited France, Switzerland and Italy gathering information for his proposed history of music. Returning home he published an account of his journey and then, in 1772, made a second tour, visiting Germany, Austria and the Low Countries. A two-volume account of his second trip, published in 1773, was followed three years later by the first of the four volumes of his 'History of Music'. His second daughter, the novelist Fanny Burney, was born while the family was living in King's Lynn.

Edward Miller was in his sixteenth year when Charles Burney left London for King's Lynn in 1751. Had he already become one of Burney's pupils before that date, or was their first meeting later in King's Lynn? Opinions differ on this. On page 59 of the 'History and Description of St. George's Church at Doncaster' (1855), by the Rev. J. E. Jackson, we are told that Miller went to London and placed himself under the instruction of the celebrated composer Dr. Burney, but the 'Dictionary of National Biography' (p.406, Vol.37) says that Miller obtained a musical training from Dr. Burney who was then at King's Lynn. No evidence is offered for either statement, indeed, very little evidence is available and that only consists of a few vague sentences found in Miller's writings. In his 'History of Doncaster', (p.309) he tells us that, 'during the latter part of Handel's life, when a boy, I used to perform on the German Flute in London, at his oratorios'. In his book 'The New Flute Instructor' we learn a little more. 'The German Flute', he writes, 'was my first instrument,' and adds that he was, 'one of the few performers now living who assisted at Handel's oratorios, during his lifetime, and constantly attended the rehearsals at his house, in Brook Street, in the Lent season'. The only date Miller gives concerning these concerts and rehearsals, also to be found in the 'History of Doncaster', is of an event which occurred, 'about 1753 in the Lent season'. It concerns a minor canon from Gloucester Cathedral who offered his services as a singer to Mr. Handel and was employed in the chorus. Not satisfied with this he requested leave to sing a solo air, that his voice might appear to more advantage. This request was also granted; but he executed his solo so little to the satisfaction of the audience that he was, to his great mortification, violently hissed. When the performance was over, by way of consolation, Handel made the following speech - 'I am sorry, very sorry for you indeed, my dear sir, but go you back to your church in de country! God will forgive you for your bad singing; dese wicked people in London, dey will not forgive you'.

Perhaps the answer to our question is that Miller studied with Burney both in London and King's Lynn. The phrase, 'when a boy' supports the view that he was in London when quite young and probably his introduction to Handel took place in the capital and was effected by the influential Burney. Miller, in the above quotations, twice refers to the 'Lent season'. Probably his visits to London were of a seasonal nature and some part of each year was spent by him in his native county where he could, between 1751 and 1756, meet Burney again and continue his studies.

It must have been some time before 1756, the year in which Miller became organist at Doncaster, that his first published work appeared — 'A Collection of New English Songs and a Cantata, set to music by

Edward Miller'. (See Appendix Five). Proof of this can be found in the list of more than two hundred subscribers which appears at the front of the book. All the addresses given are in London and East Anglia and none from Yorkshire or any other county. Moreover, one of the subscribers, the Rev. Mr. Thom, is given as Vicar of Castle Acre, a benifice which he resigned in 1756. Another subscriber, Mr. Hooke, Senior, Norwich, died in 1757. He was the father of James Hook, the celebrated organist and writer of more than two thousand songs, including 'The Lass of Richmond Hill'. Miller's collection of songs was to be had of John Johnson, the printer, at the Harp and Crown in Cheapside, and of the author at Mr. Wass's in Old Fish Street, opposite the Church. Was this Miller's London lodging? The church, St. Mary Magdalen, situated between St. Paul's and the river, was demolished in 1887. On the title-page is a notice of another recent publication - 'A Book of Short Airs or Minuets, composed for the use of young practitioners on the German Flute and Harpsichord', by Mr. Miller, Price one shilling (5p), but we have been unable to trace a copy of this work. Meanwhile the inhabitants of Doncaster were raising a subscription for the building of an organ in their parish church. This was not the church's first organ, an 'organe case' is mentioned in the 'Church Recknying' as early as 1569, but there are no records of any early instruments. On March 19th 1738-9 articles of agreement were entered into between John Harris of Red Lion Street in the parish of St. Andrew, Holborn, in the county of Middlesex, organ builder of the one part, and the Rev. Hollis Pigot, Vicar of Doncaster, William Seaton, John Hancock, James Buckley Wilsford and John Gibbons, churchwardens of the other part, for the building of an organ for the sum of 525 pounds. The Corporation agreed that, when the new organ was set up, they would pay a salary of twenty pounds a year to the organist of their appointment. The organ, built by John Byfield, brother-in-law of John Harris, was completed in 1740. Byfield was described as 'Organ builder of the parish of St. George the Martyr, now at Doncaster'. Readers are referred to Appendix Six for details of this organ, which had three manuals but no pedals. Its original position was at the entrance to the Chancel, under the central tower, in a loft to the rear of the ancient screen. A faculty for erecting a gallery, 'in the middle isle of the chancelle', is dated October 6th 1739 (Sheardown's 'Pamphlets' Vol. 1, p.52). The 'Calendar of the Records of Doncaster' (C.R.D. Vol. 4, p.227) gives the appointment of Edward Miller as organist of Doncaster on August 19th 1756 - six years after the death of Bach and three years before Handel's death - at a yearly salary of thirty pounds. Miller tells us that he obtained the appointment on the recommendation of James Nares, who had recently vacated the organ stool at York Minster on being appointed organist and composer to His Majesty's Chapel Royal in succession to Dr. Maurice Greene, deceased. The vacancy which Miller filled at Doncaster was caused by the appointment of John Camidge to succeed James Nares at York.

In the same year that Edward Miller became organist of Doncaster the burial register of St. Peter Mancroft, Norwich, has the following entry:

'1756, May 2nd, Elizabeth Miller, aged 48.'

This probably refers to Edward's mother. Eight years later, in the same register we find:

'1764, Sept. 12th, Thomas Miller from St. Giles, aged 65.'

This may be Edward's father and, if so, after Elizabeth's death he must have married again. These assumptions are based first, on an entry in the marriage registers of St. Giles' Church, Norwich:

'Thomas Miller, of this parish, widower and Tabitha Bevis, of the same, single woman, were married in this Church by Licence, this twelfth day of March in the year 1761, by me, Thomas Money, Curate.....'.

and secondly, on an administration granted in the Consistory Court of Norwich in 1764 to 'Tabitha Miller, widow, relict and administratrix of the goods, etc. of Thomas Miller, late of the parish of St. Giles, paviour, who died intestate.'

This was sworn at Norwich on September 21st 1764.

Edward Miller's Receipt for Salary as Corporation Organist.

15

Chapter Three

The Doncaster to which Edward Miller came in 1756 - the year that Mozart was born - was a town of a few thousand inhabitants which had not extended much beyond the confines of its medieval ditch. Writing thirty years earlier Defoe regarded it as - 'a spacious town, exceeding populous, and a great manufacturing town, principally for knitting; also as it stands upon the great northern post-road, it is very full of great inns.' Another writer described it as 'old knitting Doncaster' but, in emphasising this production of knitwear which, we are told, included stockings, gloves, waistcoats and petticoats, we must not forget that the main occupation of its people was that of agriculture.

The parish church of St. George stood on a small eminence to the south of the river Don and its backwater the river Cheswold, an eminence successively occupied by Roman fort and Norman motte and bailey. Outwardly the church presented a 'Perpendicular' appearance but the interior, with its 'Early English' arcading and some masonry of a still earlier period, revealed its ancient foundation. Under the shadow of its north wall stood two houses, the Vicarage and 'Church Hill', which later became Miller's home. Their gardens sloped down to the Cheswold, beyond which a marshy area stretched northward to the river Don. These two rivers met to the north-east of the church near Docken Hill, where vessels loaded and unloaded at the wharves and warehouses. From this point the Don was navigable downstream to Goole, and then Hull could be reached via the Ouse and Humber. Upstream, the river had, by 1751, been made navigable as far as Tinsley, near Sheffield. To the east and south-east of St. George's was a complex of streets and open spaces known as the Corn Market, Goose Hill and The Magdalens. The ancient Corn Market was held on the eastern side of the present Market Place and from it Soestang Lane, later known as High Fisher Gate, led past the Tithebarn and tan-yards down to Docken Hill. In the Magdalens, on part of the site of the present Market Hall, stood the Town Hall, which in its long life had undergone many changes. It was built as the Chapel of St. Mary Magdalen, being thus described in a deed of c.1174. After the dissolution of the chantries it was acquired by the civic body in 1556-7, and in addition to serving as a Town Hall it also housed the Grammar School, which shared the ground floor with several shops and the Guard Room. To the west of St. George's Church was the Great North Road which passed over Friars' Bridge and St. Mary's Bridge on its way northward. Friars' Bridge, over the River Cheswold, took its name from

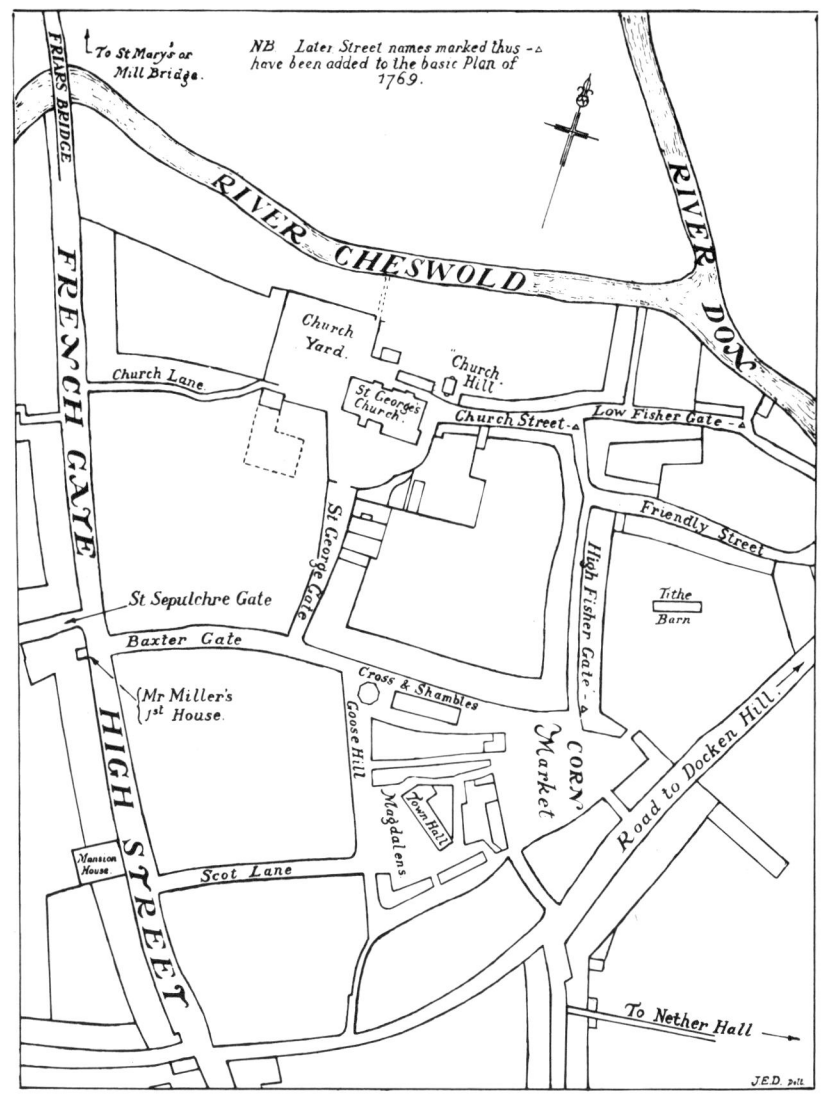

PLAN OF DONCASTER c. 1769.

the house of Franciscan or Grey Friars which formerly stood near by, whilst the ancient chapel of St. Mary was still standing on the bridge over the River Don, a little further to the north. Southwards from the church a short street known as St. George Gate joined Baxter Gate, the ancient 'Street of the Bakers'. Baxter Gate ran parallel to the church, its eastern end leading back into the market area, whilst its western end and St. Sepulchre Gate formed a cross-roads with that part of the Great North Road called High Street. It was in the High Street near to these cross-roads, which are now known as Clock Corner, that Edward Miller lived when he first came to the town. Writing of this house, he says, 'At that time my humble mansion consisted but of two rooms', and for it he paid a rent of four pounds a year. ('History of Doncaster', p. 162, note).

It was not long before he became a member of two very different organisations, one military and the other musical. The year of his arrival in the town was a disastrous one for England. The Seven Years' War began, Admiral Byng failed to relieve Minorca and was subsequently shot, the French were having successes in North America, and the country was shocked by the news of the Black Hole of Calcutta. Fear of a French invasion led Pitt the Elder, when he came to power in 1757, to reorganise the militia. The purpose of his Militia Act of that year was to give the country an adequate defence force. Each county had its quota of men to find. Lists of the able-bodied were compiled in each parish and those liable for service were selected from them by ballot. Service was for three years within this country, and the Act permitted the sending of substitutes. It appears that in some places, including Doncaster, persons were allowed to volunteer - later Acts encouraged this - and Miller tells us of sixteen men in Doncaster, of whom he was one, volunteering in 1757. Amongst them were surgeons Middleton and Farrer and also James Stovin who later became Town Clerk. The second Marquis of Rockingham was in command. A Doncaster solicitor of that time, John Ellerker, in his poem 'The Doncaster Volunteers', described satirically the activities of these patriots including the startling effect they had on Europe:

'When Britain's arms by War's fell chance
Were baffled by the arms of France,
And Louis threatened in bravado
T'invade us with a huge armado . . . . .

- - - - - -

18

At Doncaster a troop stepped forth
All men of dignity and worth,
With wrath and indignation fired,
(By Mars himself no doubt inspired),
With minds most valorous and willing
Regardless of their pay - a shilling.

- - - - - -

Soon as 'twas known they were assembled
The King of France looked pale and trembled'.....
whilst the King of Prussia said:
'Give me sixteen such as these
I'll sack Vienna when I please.'

(Doncaster Gazette, May 17th 1861).

Fortunately the invasion never took place and the services of the sixteen volunteers were not required. The enemy did, however, have one minor success, for the poem also tells of the volunteers being entertained by the Marquis at Wentworth Woodhouse. French wine proved to be their undoing and, for one night at least, they were 'hors de combat' and quite unable to return to their homes or defend their fatherland.

The other group which Edward Miller joined consisted of music-makers who met regularly at Nether Hall, the home of Robert Copley, the last of the legitimate line of the Copleys to live at this seat. The house, now used as Council offices, still stands in Nether Hall Road, but its parklands and gardens have given way to rows of terraced houses of which Copley Road is one. In his 'History of Doncaster' (p. 160-2) Miller introduces us to Robert Copley - 'Eminent as a private gentleman for his general knowledge and taste in the polite arts. In music, when at Westminster school, he was a scholar of the famous Dr. Croft, who had made him a very good performer in thorough bass on the harpsichord . . . . One day in the week, for some years, Mr. Copley appropriated to music. He had the Cooke family to dine with him, and the concert in the evening was entirely made up of performers of that family, Mr. Copley and myself excepted. Sir Brian Cooke, father of the present Sir George, performed the first violin, and the present George Cooke Yarborough, the violoncello.' Sir Brian Cooke of Wheatley Hall and George Cooke of Streetthorpe (now Edenthorpe), who assumed the name of Cooke Yarborough in 1802, were cousins.

About the year 1760, Edward Miller dined with the officers of the Durham Militia at Pontefract and, during the meal, one of them told him of a young German instrumentalist in the regimental band - but, let Miller tell the story - 'One of them informed me, that they had a young German in their band as a performer on the hautboy, who had only been a few months in this country, and yet spoke English almost as well as a native: that, exclusive of the hautboy, he was an excellent performer on the violin, and if I chose to repair to another room, he should entertain me with a solo. I did so, and Mr. Herschel executed a solo of Giardini's, in a manner that surprised me. Afterwards, I took an opportunity to have a little private conversation with him, and requested to know if he had engaged himself to the Durham Militia for any long period? He answered, "No, only from month to month". Leave them then, said I, and come and live with me. I am a single man, and I think we shall be happy together; doubtless your merit will soon entitle you to a more eligible situation. He consented to my request and came to Doncaster. It is true, at that time, my humble mansion consisted but of two rooms. However, poor as I was! my cottage contained a small library of well-chosen books; and it must appear singular, that a young German, who had been so short a time in England, should understand, even the peculiarities of our language so well, as to adopt Dean Swift for his favourite author. I took an early opportunity of introducing him at Mr. Copley's concert; ..... For never before had we heard the concertos of Corelli, Geminiani, and Avison, or the overtures of Handel, performed more chastely, or more according to the original intention of the composers, than by Mr. Herschel.' There is no doubt that the young German soon became a member of the ensemble, for Edward also says that, 'On the arrival of Mr. Herschel at Doncaster, Sir Brian Cooke, of course, resigned the first violin part to him.' ('History of Doncaster' p. 162).

On Tuesdays April 1st and 8th 1760, the 'York Courant' carried the following advertisement:

'Proposals for printing by Subscription
A Set of Lessons for the Guittar, composed in
an easy familiar Stile, natural to that Instrument.
By EDWARD MILLER, Organist at Doncaster.
Most of these lessons have an Accompanyment
for another Guittar.
Some Rules are also added for playing these
and other Lessons in Taste.
The subscription is Five Shillings, to be paid on
Delivery of the Book, which will be published as
speedily as possible.
Subscriptions are taken in at Johnson's Music Shop
in Cheapside, London; at Haxby's Music Shop in York;
and by Mr. Miller at Doncaster.
Also shortly will be published
Six Sonatas for Two Violins or German Flutes, and
a Bass. Composed by Mr. Miller.'

A few years earlier the Italian 'cetera' had been introduced to this country and become known as the English Guitar. In 1758 Robert Bremner, the Edinburgh music publisher who later became established in London, issued 'Instructions for the Guitar' in which he referred to the instrument as, 'but lately introduced into Britain.' One or two more books of instruction for playing this instrument came from other music publishers, but nothing further is known of Miller's proposals, and it is highly unlikely that either of the books mentioned in his advertisement was ever published, due no doubt to the lack of subscribers. It is perhaps because of the disappointing response to his advertisement in the 'York Courant' that he decided to launch his next work in his native county. The 'Norwich Mercury' of June 20th 1761 tells of his proposals to publish by subscription 'Six Solos for a German Flute, Hautboy or Violin, with a Thorough Bass for the Harpsichord or Violoncello', and subscribers were asked to send their names to Mr. Miller, shopkeeper in Bungay, who was, of course, Edward's brother. Delivery was promised by the end of the year and again the cost was to be five shillings (25p). This time Edward's efforts met with success and the six solos - possibly his finest work, and reminiscent of Arne - became widely known throughout the country. He preferred the word 'Opera' to 'Opus', and so describes this work as 'Opera One'. Perhaps by this time he regarded his London publications of seven or eight years before as youthful immaturities which he wished to forget, and the fact that these solos of 1761 were described as 'Opera One' is further proof that his two proposals for 1760 were never published. It is of course possible that his Opera One grew out of the proposed 'Six Sonatas for two Violins or German Flutes' of the previous year.

In his introduction to the six flute solos he writes - 'The chief Objection to the German Flute in Concert is, that it is seldom found to be well in Tune with the other Instruments; but I am much afraid this more frequently proceeds . . . . . . from the Fault of the Performer than the Instrument.' (See page 11). He suggests ways in which this faulty intonation may be overcome and then discusses the subject of tongueing - 'As it would be very difficult to execute some quick Passages with the Rapidity and Distinctness they require, by the common Method of tonguing; an Invention has been found out of sounding two Notes with one Tip of the Tongue, which the French call le double Coup de Langue, or double tonguing.' In a much later publication, his 'New Flute Instructor' of 1800, Edward tells us that the above reference to double tongueing, together with his accompanying instructions, was the first mention of this subject in any book in the English language. It is interesting also to note that the second edition of 'Six Solos for a German Flute' (1769), carried an advertisement on the title-page for German Flutes, 'with or without the Additional Keys'.

21

He was also active on the concert platform, not only performing in and around Doncaster, but also returning to his native town in order to fulfil engagements. Concerts were often a means of supplementing income, and advertisements frequently appeared with headings such as, 'For the benefit of Mr. Camidge', or 'For the benefit of Mr. Miller'. The 'Norwich Mercury' of Saturday, July 29th 1758 announced a concert of vocal and instrumental music to be held in Mr. Christien's Great Room near the Red Well, on Thursday morning, August 10th, during Assize Week, 'for the benefit of Mr. Miller and Mr. Blogg.' In addition to Mr. Miller's Solos and Concertos on the German Flute, a Miss Jennings from Doncaster was to sing, 'several favourite songs from Mr. Handel's Oratorios and Operas', and a concert was to be held for her benefit on the following morning. A return visit was made by these artists during the Assize Week of 1761, (ibid, July 4th) on the occasion of Mr. Garland's Concert of Music. Mr. Garland was the Cathedral organist, while the Mr. Blogg mentioned above was a well-known Norwich violinist who would be no stranger to Edward Miller, for the two had played together at a concert at Woodbridge in Suffolk on October 22nd 1754, almost two years before Edward came to Doncaster ('Ipswich Journal', October 19th 1754). For notices of concerts in and around Doncaster before 1786 we turn to the 'York Courant', for only a few copies survive of the local paper issued before that date ('The Sheffield Register and Doncaster Flying Post'). The 'Courant' informed its readers on Tuesday, April 15th 1760 of Mr. Miller's Subscription Concert on the following Friday evening in Doncaster Town Hall. On this occasion Miss Jennings supplemented her vocal items, which included the song 'Where the bee sucks', with a solo on the guitar, (conceivably from Miller's proposed publication. (See p. 20), and there were also solos and duets on French Horn and Bassoon. Quite often an evening concert was followed by a Ball, and this notice ended with the words, 'It will be moonlight'. A ticket for Concert and Ball generally cost half a crown (12½p). A particularly interesting advertisement appeared in the same paper on Tuesday, February 9th 1762, for it told of Mr. Miller's Concert in the Town Hall on the following Thursday with, 'the first violin by Mr. Herschell, a Native of Hanover, who will perform one of Giardini's Solos, and a Concerto on the Hautboy'.

On February 15th 1763 Mr. Edward Miller married Miss Elizabeth Lee, daughter of Thomas Lee, barber and peruke maker. The bride's great, great, great grandfather, also called Thomas Lee, and a tanner by trade, was an Alderman, Justice of the Peace, and in 1633 and part of 1638, Mayor of Doncaster. In the same year, on May 13th 1763 it was ordered 'that if Mr. Miller, the organist will undertake to instruct the Corporation band of music to play upon the hautboy and bassoon, the Corporation will be at the expense of the instruments'. (C.R.D. Vol. 4,

TOWN HALL AND THEATRE.
From Miller's 'History of Doncaster'.

p. 232). That he undertook this task is shown by the following bill in the Corporation Accounts:

		London, 1763				
Mr. Edward Miller		Bo^t of Caleb Gedney				
June 20th		£.		s.		d
A Bassoon & Crook		5	,,	5	,,	0
A Reed Case for Ditto		0	,,	3	,,	6
Six Reeds For Ditto		0	,,	9	,,	0
Two plain Hoboys		2	,,	12	,,	0
Two Reed Cases for Ditto		0	,,	6	,,	0
Twelve Reeds for Ditto		0	,,	12	,,	0
A Book of Instructions, Hoboy		0	,,	1	,,	6
A Scale for the Bassoon		0	,,	1	,,	6
		£9	,,	10	,,	6

The Corporation Receipts for July 6th of that year record the payment to Edward Miller of the £9 ,, 10 ,, 6 (£9.52½) and Mr. Henry Heaton, Carrier, Fisher Gate, received one shilling (5p) for the carriage of the instruments from London in one of his stage waggons. About this time it was possible to travel from York and Doncaster to London on 'Flying Post Coaches with Steel Springs'. Leaving York at 4 a.m. and calling at Doncaster, an overnight stop was made at Grantham, and London was reached the following evening. Six inside passengers could be carried and each paid threepence a mile. Stage waggons, carrying goods and also passengers at a cheaper rate, took about six days to do the same journey. The Corporation Waits were an institution of some antiquity, the first known reference to the appointment of 'pipers or waits' occurred in 1457 when Alan and William Pyper were elected to that office. In later years the number of players was increased to three or four, each being provided with a hat and a scarlet cloak of the Corporation livery. Not all the members of the 'Town's Musick' were pipers. On April 11th 1749 it was ordered that, 'Mr. Newbold be employed to get Mr. Bonnington a new or second hand bass viol, and that twenty shillings be deducted out of his salary every year till the money be paid'. (C.R.D. Vol. 4, p. 221). In August 1760, the players were described as 'waits or fiddlers'.

On December 28th 1763 the Millers' firstborn, Thomas, was baptized but only lived a few months. Thereafter there was a newcomer to the family almost yearly until Mrs. Miller died after ten and a half years of married life. During that time she had borne three boys and seven girls, but of these, only the third child, William Edward (1766-

1839) reached mature years (See Appendix Two). Most probably Edward's marriage, and the arrival of children, forced him to quit his 'humble mansion' and, according to Hatfield ('Historical Notices of Doncaster', 1866, Vol. 1, p. 381) he moved to 'Church Hill' in 1765, where he lived for the rest of his life. Now known as 'St. George House' or 'Clergy House', 'Church Hill' still stands to the north of the church and has that name engraved on a gatepost. It is one of the oldest inhabited houses in Doncaster, for it was not new when the Millers went there. At that time it had a long garden at the rear which sloped down to the river Cheswold, but it was not then the detached residence it is today. Huddled against its eastern wall was a number of small dwellings, out-buildings and workrooms, which surrounded an open space or yard. Hatfield gives the following entry from the Poor Rate of 1765 -

'Fisher Gate -Mr. Miller, for late Mr. Godmond's
School and 4 tenements, yearly rent
£8 ,, 10 ,, 0. (£8.50)
Mr. Miller, for Wm. Busby's house £2 '.
('Historical Notices of Doncaster', Vol. 1, p. 381)

It is almost certain that the building used as a school by the Reverend Mr. Godmond was the house 'Church Hill', and most probably the tenements were in the adjoining yard, which became known as 'Miller's Yard'. This property came into Edward Miller's possession on his marriage to Elizabeth Lee, for it had previously belonged to her father. Indeed, the land upon which 'Church Hill' was built about the middle of the eighteenth century, had been in the Lee family since Thomas Lee, tanner, who became Mayor and Justice of the Peace, acquired it in 1620. (Doncaster Archives, 'Indenture of Sale' dated October 9th 1620). A later indenture, dated June 21st 1765, in describing the boundaries of premises between Fisher Gate and the river Cheswold, to be leased by Mr. Solomon Holmes, fellmonger, states that towards the west they 'abut upon the ground belonging to Mr. Edward Miller, formerly the estate of Mr. Thomas Lee'. (Deed Number 928, Doncaster Archives).

The following entries in the registers of St. George's Church refer to Elizabeth's parents. The burial of Diana, wife of Thomas Lee is recorded on April 15th 1748 and in the following year on April 23rd, Thomas Lee was buried. Thus Elizabeth, who was born on August 8th 1745 was orphaned in infancy.

Her father's Will, dated March 23rd 1748-9, is recited in part in an Assignment of Lease dated September 19th 1749. (Doncaster Archives - Envelope J9-19). In it he leaves his property in trust for his daughter

Elizabeth until she reaches the age of twenty-one, or until she be married, which event should happen first.

Before the nineteenth century the term 'Fisher Gate' was loosely applied to a district to the north-east of the Parish Church, in which were certain portions of the ancient church-yard and several streets later known as High Fishergate, Low Fishergate, Church Street and Friendly Street. The first known mention of Church Street is in 1796, while the distinction between High and Low Fishergate did not appear until a little later.

'CHURCH HILL' LOOKING NORTH, 1975.
Photograph - G. Swann.

Chapter Four

In 1765 the musical gatherings at Nether Hall ceased because of the illness of Robert Copley, an illness which ended with his death in 1771. In his 'History of Doncaster' (p. 163) Miller says that 'For the last six years of Mr. Copley's life, a lamentable change took place. He became a prey to the deepest melancholy, and was tormented by an idea, that the French would invade and conquer England; deprive him of all his property, and that he should be reduced to real want before he died. Previous to this change in his disposition, he might truly have been stiled the Mecaenas of Doncaster. Delighting in the society of men of genius, such characters ever found an easy access to Nether Hall, where he kept an hospitable table from which the poor were daily fed.' Among the men of genius who visited Nether Hall were Thomas Gray and his friend the Reverend William Mason. Gray had already polished, repolished and published his famous 'Elegy written in a Country Churchyard', and had also refused the Poet Laureateship. That Mason was also regarded as a poet is shown by his memorial in the Poets' Corner at Westminster Abbey. The two advised each other on their writings but, whereas Gray's verse still lives, Mason's is almost forgotten. A person of great activity, widely known and respected in many fields, William Mason was an example of the better kind of pluralist. Baptized at Holy Trinity Church, Hull, in 1725, he was ordained in 1754, and from that year until his death in 1797, was Rector of Aston, near Sheffield. That, however, was only one of his many posts. From 1754 to 1761 he was Chaplain to Lord Holderness. As Royal Chaplain to Georges II and III (1757 - 1772), he resided at Court for a month each year, and was also required to live at York for several months annually where he was Canon Residentiary and Precentor at the Minster (1762 - 1797). He still found time, however, to write hymns for his parish, anthems for the Minster, essays and verse, and also verse-plays which were performed at Covent Garden. In addition he was an authority on landscape gardening, an amateur painter, and the inventor of a musical instrument known as the celestinette. One wonders if this was the same as the 'newly invented instrument called the celestion d'amour' advertised by Mr. Thomas Haxby, music and musical instrument dealer, in the 'York Courant' of Tuesday, August 19th 1766. Edward Miller dedicated his Opera Terza to Mason and attempted to teach him musical composition, but afterwards admitted that he had little success. Gray bequeathed his library and all his papers to Mason including the original manuscript of the 'Elegy'. In 1775, four years after Gray's death, he published 'The Poems of

NETHER HALL, NEAR DONCASTER.
The Seat of Robert Copley, Esq.

Mr. Gray, to which are prefixed Memoirs of his Life and Writings'. It is chiefly by this work that Mason is remembered, for he was the pioneer of the writing of biography through 'life and letters'. In his book, 'The Development of English Biography' (Hogarth Lecture on Literature, No. 4, Hogarth Press, 1927), Harold Nicolson remarks that, 'Mason, almost by chance, hit upon a method which rendered possible the technique of biography as we know it today'.

About the time that the music-making at Nether Hall was ending, the celebrated organ builder, Johann Snetzler, was building a new organ in the Parish Church of Halifax. William Herschel was one of the seven candidates seeking the position of organist, and at the interview the seven drew lots to determine the order in which they were to show their capabilities on the new instrument. Edward Miller travelled with his friend to this audition and gives a most interesting account in his 'History of Doncaster', (p. 162, note) of what happened. This new organ had, of course, no pedals -

'My friend Herschel drew the third lot - the second performer was Mr. Wainwright, afterwards Dr. Wainwright, of Manchester, whose finger was so rapid, that old Snetzler, the organ-builder, ran about the church exclaiming, "te tevel, te tevel, he run over te key like one cat, he vil not give my piphes room for to shpeak." During Mr. Wainwright's performance, I was standing in the middle ile with Herschel. What chance have you, said I, to follow this man? He replied, "I don't know; I am sure fingers will not do." On which, he ascended the organ loft, and produced from the organ, so uncommon a fulness - such a volume of slow solemn harmony, that I could by no means account for the effect. After this short extempore effusion, he finished with the old-hundredth psalm tune, which he played better than his opponent. "Aye, aye", cried old Snetzler, "tish is very goot, very goot indeed, I vil luf tish man, for he gives my piphes room for to shpeak." Having, afterwards, asked Mr. Herschel by what means, in the beginning of his performance, he produced so uncommon an effect? He replied, "I told you fingers would not do," and producing two pieces of lead from his waistcoat pocket. "One of these", said he, "I placed on the lowest key of the organ, and the other upon the octave above: thus, by accommodating the harmony, I produced the effect of four hands instead of two. However, as my leading the concert on the violin, is their principal object, they will give me the place in preference to a better performer on the organ; but I shall not stay long here, for I have the offer of a superior situation at Bath, which offer I shall accept." '

Miller does not give a date for the above happening but the 'Dictionary of National Biography' (p. 207, Vol. 53) states that Johann

Snetzler built the Halifax organ in 1766, a statement confirmed by a notice in the 'York Courant' on August 5th of that year, which announced the opening of the new organ in Halifax Parish Church on Thursday and Friday, August the 28th and 29th. There were to be performances of 'Messiah' each morning at half past ten with an Organ-Concerto, 'between Acts one and two'. The advertisement added that, 'An Organist is wanted'. Previously Snetzler had been employed on the Doncaster organ, as the following receipt shows, - 'April 26th, 1758. Received of Mr. Francis Caley, churchwarden, the sum of Twenty Pounds for Repairing and Tuneing the Organ - by me - John Snetzler'.

Herschel, true to his word, stayed only a brief period in Halifax before moving to Bath, where the duties of Organist at the Octagon Chapel, together with teaching, composing and the directing of concerts kept him fully occupied for many years. Perhaps 'fully occupied' is an exaggeration, for he was a person of wide interests who gradually became more and more absorbed in the study of astronomy and optics. His appointment as Court Astronomer in 1782 relieved him of the necessity of earning his living by music. He had, by that time, achieved fame for his discoveries including that of the Planet Uranus, and also for the construction of large telescopes. His life became devoted to a thorough examination of the heavens and to making still further improvements to the essential instruments. Thus the young musician from Germany, the fourth son of a bandmaster in the Hanoverian Guard, who was happy to come to Doncaster and share Edward Miller's 'humble mansion', became famous, not for his music, but as one of our great pioneers in physical astronomy. He received a knighthood in 1816, which was only one of the many honours bestowed upon him.

About the time when Herschel left Doncaster it appears that Edward Miller was in financial difficulty. He had a wife and two children to support, one child having died, and it is possible that he appealed to the Corporation, for the 'Calendar' records that from the 8th April 1767 his salary was to be increased to forty guineas (£42) a year, 'in consideration of the dearness of provisions and of his business as a teacher of music having declined' (C.R.D. Vol. 4, p. 238). His fourth child, Sarah, was born in October 1767 but only lived a few months. On November 24th of that year an advertisement in the 'York Courant' told of Edward's proposals for publishing by subscription his 'Six Sonatas or Lessons for the Harpsichord.' Subscribers were asked to leave their names with Mr. Welcker, the printer, in Gerrard Street, St. Ann's Soho, or with Mr. Bremner in the Strand, or Mrs. Johnson in Cheapside. Country subscribers could contact Mr. Haxby or Mr. Shaw in York, Mr. Chase in Norwich, Mr. Wynne in Cambridge, or the author in Doncaster. The book, costing six shillings (30p), was promised for December, but

Edward's forecasts of publication dates were generally far too optimistic, and most probably at least a year elapsed before subscribers received their copies. A footnote to the advertisement mentions a book of 'Odes and Songs' which the author hoped to publish in December 1768 at the price of half a guinea (52½p) but, as we shall see later, this work did not appear before 1770 or 1771. The 'Six Sonatas for the Harpsichord'became Miller's 'Opera Seconda'. Each piece consists of two or three short movements - 'Allegro and Minuet'; 'Largo and Air with Variations'; 'Allegro, Largo and Rondeau' for example - and the last three Sonatas have parts for the Violin or German Flute. Though some of the movements have a certain charm, the work as a whole does not reach the heights of the flute solos of 'Opera One'.

In the August and September of 1768 a concert notice headed 'Doncaster Races' appeared in three issues of the 'York Courant'. The town's association with horse-racing goes back for hundreds of years and, by the early eighteenth century, the Corporation was making a monetary grant towards the meetings, which were held annually and varied from two to five days in length. By the middle of that century September had become the recognised month for this event. In 1766 the Doncaster Gold Cup was instituted and ten years later, at Colonel Anthony St. Leger's suggestion, a race for three-year-olds was established. Also in that year, 1776, the Corporation ordered the setting out of a new course on Doncaster Common and the building of a commodious stand (C.R.D. Vol. 4, p. 248). Thus the race-course came to its present position and a stand, unfortunately no longer in existence, was designed by John Carr. Two years later, the race for three-year-olds became known as the 'St. Leger'. During the meetings the local hotels, inns and lodging-houses were full, and in addition to afternoons devoted to racing, other social attractions had to be provided. In his 'History of Doncaster', (p. 158) Miller tells us that in the mornings the gentlemen's time was usually employed in hunting, and every evening there was a Play at the Theatre and a Ball at the Mansion House. No doubt, there were many visitors to whom a morning's hunting made no appeal, and so quite often a musical alternative was offered either in the Parish Church or Mansion House. Programmes varied considerably from year to year, and the occasional absence of advertisements suggests that in some years there were no Race Week concerts. In 1768 Handel's Oratorio 'Judas Maccabeus' was performed by eighty vocalists and instrumentalists under the direction of Edward Miller in the church at 10 a.m. on Tuesday September 20th, and 'Messiah' the following morning. Tickets cost five shillings and half a crown (12½p). In less ambitious years there was perhaps only one concert during Race Week, given by a few artists and without choir or orchestra, very similar in nature to the 'benefit' concerts already mentioned, but which cannot all be recorded here. Perhaps one exception may be made and the concert, 'For the benefit of Mr. Jobson, organist, Wakefield', included briefly. Advertised in the 'Courant' of Tuesday May 13th 1766, it was held on the following Friday at 7 p.m. in the Wakefield Assembly Rooms. Picture our Mr. Miller setting out on a beautiful Spring morning to ride the twenty miles through a countryside as yet unspoilt by pit heaps, power stations, railway viaducts or motorways, humming or whistling a phrase from the Concerto which he was to play on the flute that evening, and looking forward to enjoying the Minuets, Gavottes and other dances of the Ball to follow.

In 1769 the music of Race Week occupied three mornings and the event was closely connected with the 'Odes and Songs' already advertised but not yet forthcoming. The 'York Courant' of September 5th and 12th 1769 announced 'A Concerto Spirituale, after the manner of the Italians, will be performed in the Church at Doncaster on Wednesday September 27th, by a select and numerous Band of Vocal and Instrumental performers, in which will be introduced (for the first time in this part of the country) the celebrated "Funeral Anthem for Queen Caroline", as performed at Westminster Abbey, composed by Mr. Handel. An Ode of Mr. Pope's intitled "The Dying Christian to his soul"; and an "Elegy on the Death of Mr. Handel", the music of both being composed by Mr. Miller'. This was to be repeated on the Friday, with Handel's 'Acis and Galatea' in the Town Hall on the Thursday, performances each day being at eleven. The advertisement ended with a further appeal:

'Proposals for printing by Subscription a Collection of Elegies, Odes and Songs. The Music composed by Edward Miller of Doncaster. The Subscription of half a guinea to be paid on delivery of the book, which will be certainly in March, 1770.'

When this work finally appeared, its list of two hundred subscribers included the names of Dr. Burney; Miss Burney; Dr. Boyce, Composer and Master of His Majesty's Band of Music; Mr. Snetzler, organ builder; The Musical Society of Doncaster; George Cooke of Street-thorpe, the violoncello player; and Thomas Copley, the natural son of Miller's host at Nether Hall. In his preface Miller attacks the vocal gymnastics so fashionable in the first half of the eighteenth century - 'The author has not written it according to the present fashionable Mode. He cannot approve a Stile which appears to him more calculated to display the Vanity of the Singers than to do Justice to the Sentiments of the Poet. To please those Public Warblers, what a quantity of trifling Composition has been obtruded on the World, and how soon sunk into Oblivion.' He gives advice to 'young Composers like myself', stressing the necessity for them 'to study Simplicity of Stile, and forget the Ostentation and Parade of Art.' In this collection there are seven soprano songs with instrumental accompaniment. One of them has words 'wrote by Colonel Lovelace in Prison, 1648', and includes the oft-quoted lines, 'Stone Walls does not a Prison make, Nor Iron Bars a Cage.' The Ode by Mr. Pope, performed in the 1769 concert, and also found in the book, opens with the lines, 'Vital Spark of Heav'nly Flame, quit, Oh! quit this Mortal Frame.' Also included are the 'Elegy on the Death of Mr. Handel' and 'The Sweet Neglect' with words by Ben Johnson *(sic)*. This work, dedicated to the Rev. Mr. Mason, became Miller's 'Opera Terza'.

A page from Miller's 'Elegies' (Op. 3).

Chapter Five

Elizabeth Miller died on August 14th 1773 at the age of 28. On the day she was buried, August 18th, her daughter Jane was baptized. She had been married for less than eleven years and in that time had borne ten children, three boys and seven girls. Three of the children, Thomas, Sarah and Diana, predeceased her, Alice outlived her mother by less than five months, and it is believed that Jane also died when very young, for nothing more is known of her. Thus Edward, at the age of 38, was left with the remaining five children - Lois, a second Thomas, Mary, William Edward and Elizabeth, aged 1, 3, 4, 7 and 8 years respectively. What help he had in the daily round of household duties, and with the care and upbringing of his young family we do not know. Perhaps some unknown person gave long and devoted service, or there may have been a succession of housekeeper-foster-mothers, some soon tiring of their arduous duties, others proving unsatisfactory. It is tempting to speculate further and imagine help coming from Norwich. Perhaps one of his sisters came to his aid, or was the mother's place occupied for part of the time at least by Elizabeth Brailsford, whom we shall meet later in this chapter? This however, can only be conjecture, for Edward remains silent on the subject. Most probably his music left him little time for domestic duties. His church and civic work may not have been too onerous but his musical activities were many and varied. In addition to his private pupils it is most likely that by this time he was teaching music classes in a young ladies' seminary. There were concert performances too, not only in the neighbourhood of Doncaster, but in other counties and even as far afield as the East Anglia of his boyhood. The 'York Courant' announced a Festival in the church at East Retford in 1771. On Monday morning, August 5th, at eleven, 'Judas Maccabeus' was performed, 'Messiah' on the Tuesday morning and 'Acis and Galatea' in the Town Hall on Tuesday evening - 'the whole to be conducted by Mr. Miller who will play a Concerto on the organ, which is now repairing, an additional stop added and a great improvement made. To add to the solemnity of the Oratorios the Chorus Singers will appear in surplices.' In 1772 the 'Ipswich Journal' announced special services on Sunday, October 11th at St. James' Church in the morning and St. Mary's in the afternoon for the benefit of the charity children of that town. During the services an anthem would be performed that had been 'composed for this occasion by Mr. Miller of Doncaster, who will play the organ.' This reminds us that Edward devoted some time to the composing of songs and anthems, and the writing of his major works with all the essential preparation and research, would also be time consuming. In the early 1770's he was also embarking on yet another activity which can scarcely be regarded as musical, for, in a modest way, he added farming to his other pursuits!

To the south of Doncaster there was a large area of undrained fenland known as Potteric Carr. It stretched for about four miles and was bordered by the villages of Balby, Cantley, Loversall and Wadworth. Within this marshy tract lay the Doncaster Corporation's Decoy where wild fowl were netted, and there was at least one expanse of deep water from which pike and eels were taken.

In the year 1765 an Act of Parliament was obtained for the draining, dividing and enclosing of this area. Each freeholder in Doncaster and the above named villages was to have a piece of land allotted, its size depending on the extent of his freehold property. Three large drains, fourteen feet wide and four miles long, were cut to take the water southwards to Rossington Bridge, below which they joined the river Torne on its way to the Trent.

Edward Miller tells us, in his 'History of Doncaster' (p. 200) of his venture into husbandry - 'Soon after the Act was obtained, and the drainage commenced, I rented of the Corporation of Doncaster sixty-five acres of this land, and had a lease for twenty-one years, on an average at nine shillings (45p) an acre.' (C.R.D. Vol. 1, p. 125, Sept. 14th 1772 - Indenture of Lease by Mayor, Aldermen and Burgesses to Edward Miller for 21 years of a close on Doncaster Carr and two closes on Balby Carr at a yearly rental of £30-16-0) (£30.80). 'At the expiration of the lease, the corporation let it for more than treble the price they had formerly received. I purchased of private persons, twenty acres of Potteric Car in its original state for about seven pounds per acre, and sold it afterwards for forty pounds.

In order to improve this land, my first process was to pare and burn the soil; but on ploughing the land afterwards for a crop of rape, the horses sunk up to the middle, and my men were often seen drawing their legs out of the bog with ropes. I also lost two or three horses, which were drowned in the drains by attempting to drink, where the ground was so boggy that they could not obtain foot-hold.

After a tolerable crop of rape, I was encouraged to try wheat; but had only a single sack from ten acres: for though the wheat looked so green and well in the month of April, that three pounds an acre were offered for the crop, yet, after that period, the blade turned yellow and curled, there being no stability of soil to nourish the plants: thus, in

August, scarcely any wheat was to be seen, but a plentiful crop of rushes, or what is here called car thack, succeeded; so that except the single sack of wheat just mentioned, the only produce I reaped was some course litter for my horses.'

Such were our organist's experiences on Potteric Carr in the early days of its enclosure, but gradually the difficulties that he and the other pioneers encountered were overcome, and he was able to report the change that had taken place by the time he was writing his 'History of Doncaster' (p. 202) towards the end of the century -

'The present occupiers, however, have a much better chance of success. The soil is now become more compact - the horses can plough without sinking - good crops of rape, oats, and wheat have lately been procured; and such parts of it as have been sown with grass seeds are now become excellent pasturage for cattle, especially for milk cows. A variety of manures has been tried on Potteric Car; but upon this kind of peat earth, those manures succeed the best, which tend to fasten the soil, and render it more compact and solid; such as the scrapings of the limestone road between Doncaster and Balby. Even common sand, or coal ashes are, of more use than rich stable dung, which passes through this kind of soil like a sieve, without adhering to its surface.'

Shortly after acquiring his land Edward built a house upon it which is still standing and occupied, and known as Carr Grange. It is assumed that this was built for his farm overseer, for he himself was still living at 'Church Hill' which continued to be his home for the rest of his life.

Not long after the death of his wife another woman came into his life, another Elizabeth in fact. The reader has already met four Elizabeths -Edward's mother, his sister, his wife and daughter - and now a fifth appears in the person of Elizabeth Brailsford. Very little is known about her. The Doncaster parish registers have been searched in vain for information concerning her birth or baptism, and consequently she cannot be linked with other Brailsfords in the town. Her name does appear in the burial registers however, her death occurring on November 22nd 1843 at the age of 88, and so she was most probably born in 1755. When she was about 22 years old she gave birth to a boy - Isaac Brailsford. This child does not appear in the register of baptisms either, but again the burial registers are more helpful. He died on July 29th 1842, aged 64, which indicates he was born in 1777 or 1778. His father was Edward Miller.

There is no direct evidence for this assertion, but the following facts are convincing:

The Doncaster parish register of baptisms records the baptism on August 1st 1785 of 'Edward Brailsford base son of Elizabeth Brailsford, Edward Miller, reputed father.'

The Clerk's rough register for that year is still in existence and contains a similar entry to that just given, but adds the word 'Organist' after Edward Miller's name.

Both Isaac and Edward Brailsford were beneficiaries under Edward Miller's Will to the extent of receiving £300 each, subject to certain conditions.

Isaac Brailsford received an education in which music featured prominently, and for six years he was a chorister of His Majesty's Chapel Royal. Later he became organist of Bradford, and on Edward Miller's death succeeded him as organist of Doncaster.

Thus there is little doubt that Edward Miller was the father of both the Brailsfords, and it is quite possible that Elizabeth Brailsford, who was about eighteen years of age when Mrs. Miller died, was for some time at least, Edward's housekeeper and the foster-mother to his young children. She is almost certainly the Elizabeth Brailsford, aged 85, Grocer, of Fisher Gate, recorded in the census of 1841.

CARR GRANGE, 1976.

37

Chapter Six

Wentworth Woodhouse, one of the largest of our stately homes, stands in undulating and well-wooded country about four miles north-west of Rotherham. Nearby is Wentworth village, rural, peaceful, dreaming of years gone by, and surrounded by factories, furnaces, pit-heads and power stations which, fortunately, it cannot see. There were Winteworths or Wentworths in this part of Yorkshire as early as the fourteenth century and their descendants are still there. Probably the most famous Wentworth was Thomas, born in Chancery Lane, London, on the Good Friday of 1593. Much of his boyhood was spent in Yorkshire. He was knighted at the age of 18, and by the time he was 21 had inherited the estates and become a Member of Parliament. His rise to power continued - Viscount; Privy Councillor; President of the Council of the North; Lord Deputy of Ireland; Commander in Chief of the Army and first Earl of Strafford. As adviser to His Majesty King Charles I he was one of the most powerful men in the land, but eventually he shared the growing unpopularity of his royal master and suffered the same fate. On May 12th 1641 large crowds assembled on Tower Hill to see him meet his death on the block. His son William, who succeeded him as second Earl of Strafford, died without issue in 1695 and the estate passed to his nephew, Thomas Watson, a son of his sister who had married Edward, second Baron Rockingham, of Rockingham Castle, Northamptonshire. This Thomas assumed the surname of Wentworth, and when he died in 1723 was succeeded by his only son, also Thomas Watson-Wentworth, who later became the first Marquis of Rockingham. During his lifetime the present house took shape. About 1725 he commenced the building of the West Front, and on its completion some seven or eight years later, turned his attention to the East Front, six hundred feet in length, thus completely engulfing the earlier residence. He died in 1750, the house still far from finished, and was succeeded by his fifth and youngest son, Charles.

Charles Watson-Wentworth, second Marquis of Rockingham, Knight of the Garter, leader of the Whig Party, First Lord of the Treasury (Prime Minister) in two governments, and a prominent figure in the sporting world - tradition says that it was he who gave the name to the St. Leger race - has never been forgotten in his native county. The numerous Rockingham roads and streets, the Rockingham clubs and 'pubs' still found in South Yorkshire testify to this, and we may add such varied objects as pottery and porcelain, a very early steam-powered ship, and a hymn-tune which were all named after this respected and popular person. The hymn-tune was a small tribute by Edward Miller who had known the Marquis since his militia days. This was not his only tribute to the man whom he regarded as his patron and to whom he felt much indebted. Writing in his 'History of Doncaster' (p. 367, note) some time after Rockingham's death in 1782, he says:

'However vain it may appear, gratitude impels me to say, that in the late most noble Marquis of Rockingham, I ever found a kind and zealous patron. When the place of master of his Majesty's Band of musicians was vacant by the death of Dr. Boyce, his Lordship applied to the Duke of Manchester, Lord Chamberlain of the Household, in whose gift it was, and requested him to appoint me his successor. I was soon honored with a letter from the Duke, (which I have now in my possession) saying, that from Lord Rockingham's recommendation, he certainly would have given me the place, had not his Majesty particularly desired him to bestow it on Mr. Stanley, the celebrated blind performer on the organ.' Miller gives no date but the above must have happened in 1779, the year when Dr. William Boyce died and John Stanley became Master of the King's Band.

Three years later Edward Miller, still seeking a royal appointment, tried again, as the following letter from the Wentworth Woodhouse Papers shows. It was addressed to the Rev. Mr. King, Secretary to the most Noble, the Marquiss of Rockingham, and dated June 9th 1782.

Rev^d. Sir,

I beg leave to return you my most grateful acknowledgement for your polite, and obliging deportment to my Sister, on her application for me to succeed Mr. Wiedeman as Director of the Music at the Court Balls, & which place is in the disposal of the Duke of Manchester.

The many proofs I have had of Lord Rockingham's goodness to me, I hope will plead for my presumption in writing to him, & his condescension in wishing to serve me now, has imprest me with such gratitude, as can never expire but with my breath.

I feel the force of his Lordship's remark that the Queen might rather wish for a German to be appointed, but as the place is entirely in the Duke of Manchester's department, it is highly probable her Majesty may not chuse to Interfere, at least I hope so: And that she may not, I have some reason to expect Lady Charlotte Fynch will apply to her for that purpose - In case her Majesty does not Interfere, there is one reason/however it may appear trifling to others/will have great weight with a Mason. The Duke of Manchester is our Grand Master & constituted a Lodge of Masons at Doncaster of which I am an officer; and on masonic principles, provided the Candidates are all in other respects equal to him, he will probably chuse to give the Preference to a Mason - and should her Majesty require a German to succeed Mr. Wiedeman, the Duke of Manchester, by a word from my Lord, would put me down in his List, for the next Vacancy in the King's Band, which though only 40£ p. Annum, is an object for me & my family, & which place can only be supplied by an Englishman. Please to make known to my Lord, the warm effusions of a grateful heart for his goodness, & accept my sincere thanks to you for your politeness to my Sister.

Believe me Rev^d. Sir

Y^r. most oblig'd & obedient Servant

Edwd. Miller

(Wentworth Woodhouse Muniments, R108/69, Sheffield City Library - with acknowledgements to Earl Fitzwilliam and his Trustees, and to the Director of the Library.)

It is not known which of Miller's sisters was involved, nor why this indirect manner of approach was used. In the March of 1782 Rockingham had again become First Lord of the Treasury and most probably saw little of his house at Wentworth. Perhaps the sister concerned lived in or near London and could more readily approach His Lordship's secretary. This secretary, the Rev. Mr. King, was the Rev. Walker King who later became Bishop of Rochester. His brother Capt. James King R.N. accompanied Capt. Cook on his last expedition, and after Cook's tragic death assisted in preparing the journal of the voyage for publication, writing the final volume himself. It is interesting to note that Fanny Burney's brother James was also serving with Cook when he died.

The 'Lady Charlotte Fynch' mentioned in the letter was Lord Rockingham's cousin, his mother being Lady Mary Finch, daughter of the 6th Earl of Winchilsea. The King's Band of Musicians was a very ancient foundation which Grove's 'Dictionary' traces back as far as Edward IV who had thirteen minstrels - 'whereof some be trumpets, some with shalmes and small pypes.' During some reigns a 'Queen's Band' also existed and it was most probably this body which provided the music at the Court Balls. Mr. Wiedeman was a distinguished flautist who was one of the founders of the Society of Musicians in London. The St. George's Lodge of Free and Accepted Masons (No. 242) was constituted at Doncaster on July 12th 1780 and Edward Miller was Worshipful

Master in 1786 and also for a very lengthy period from 1792 to 1801. His portrait was presented to the Lodge in 1795.

Within a few weeks of the writing of the above letter the Marquis died while still in office, and no more is heard of Miller's desires for a court appointment. On hearing of the death of his patron he immediately wrote a more ambitious tribute, a 28-page booklet, printed by C. Plummer, Frenchgate, Doncaster, and called 'The Tears of Yorkshire for the Loss of the Most Noble the Marquis of Rockingham.' The sub-title sums up the contents of this eulogy - 'The History of his Life and Death, to which is added An Account of his Funeral; the Particulars of his Will and his Character.' In his 'History of Doncaster', (p. 367, note) Miller says that on the day of the Marquis's interment in York Minster, 'six hundred copies of this literary trifle were sold in the course of a few hours.'

In the year following this tribute to 'The Glory of Yorkshire' - as the author described the late Marquis on the final page - one of Miller's major works was published. 'The Dictionary of National Biography' (p. 406, Vol. 37) gives the date of 1771 for his 'Opera Four', but there is no doubt that it did not appear until twelve years later. On Tuesday, February 18th 1783, the 'York Courant' announced publication that day of 'Institutes of Music, or An Easy Introduction to the Harpsichord, by Edward Miller, Organist at Doncaster.' The printers were Longman and Broderip of number 26, Cheapside and 13, Haymarket, London, and the price of a copy was ten shillings and sixpence (52½p). The firm of Longman and Broderip was not established until 1776 and they did not acquire their Haymarket premises until the December of 1782. The rather grandiose title of this work reminds us of former meanings of the verb 'to institute', which include 'to teach, to train, to ground, to instruct and to educate'. A lengthy sub-title informed the reader that 'everything necessary for well-grounding the Scholar in the Rudiments of the Science is fully treated of in a new and familiar Manner by Question and Answer. To which are added easy and pleasant lessons for Practice, properly fingered for young Beginners - Part composed and Part selected from the works of the best masters.' The demand for this tutor must have been immediate and encouraging, for only a few weeks later the 'Norwich Mercury' of Tuesday March 22nd 1783 notified its readers that, 'This day is published a Second Impression (the first being all sold in a few days) of "Institutes of Music", by Edward Miller.' Less than two and a half years later, the same paper told on August 6th 1785 of 'A new edition, being the fifth, of "Institutes of Music"'. Unfortunately we do not know what is meant in these two Norwich advertisements by the terms 'impression' and 'edition'.

In the preface to the 'Institutes' the author gives his reasons for undertaking the work - quite a substantial volume of about seventy large pages - and also explains its purpose:

'It is a common observation that young ladies at Boarding-Schools seldom make great progress at Music. The author, many years employed at such seminaries, is convinced of the truth of such remarks, and at the same time conscious that the difficulty of redressing it arises out of the shortness of time a master can allow each scholar when there are numbers to be taught . . . . . .

After many experiments the author has found that the best method of communicating the principles of music to young students is by Question and Answer. Thus, if twenty young ladies learn music at the same school, which is not uncommon, suppose instead of one being taught the usual time, and then another called to take her place, the whole number were collected together, and while one is performing on the harpsichord, the rest are usefully employed in learning the Elements of Music - some the names and lengths of the notes, some the different Characters, some in counting time, others copying music etc, all of which may be done with very little trouble to the Master, for while he is engaged with ONE at the harpsichord, the rest may be questioning and assisting each other in the principles of the Science here laid down. They must doubtless learn more in one lesson than by several in the common way.'

Teaching aids, in the form of music tutor books for schools and young persons, must have been hitherto unknown and likely to be regarded with some suspicion - was 'Institutes of Music' the first-ever School Music Book, and the first instrumental Tutor written expressly for children, in the English language? - for Edward concludes his Preface by addressing himself to his colleagues and assuring them that by adopting his book they have much to gain and nothing to fear:

'It is to be hoped the judicious and candid Master, if he assent to the truth of the above remarks, will have no objection to a Plan, which will save him much trouble in writing for his Scholars. If many are to be taught his task is not easy. No aid is to be slighted - Every assistance is to be wished for; and surely the use of this Book can no more affect his importance, than that of a Teacher of a Language is lessened, by making use of Grammars, and other means of assistance for young beginners.'

Thus we can picture him at work in a young ladies' seminary nearly two hundred years ago. The girls, with one exception, are sitting about the room with their copies of the 'Institutes' opened at some lesson or other in Part One - more than twenty pages of theory or 'Elements of

Music', from the names of the lines and spaces to the major and minor modes, ornaments and transposition. Apart from some musical examples in the text the information is 'communicated to the young students' almost entirely by means of Question and Answer, as shown by these opening lines of Part One, Chapter One, Lesson One:

'PUPIL.   How many letters are made use of in Music?
MASTER. Seven.
P.   Which are they?
M.   A.B.C.D.E.F.G. and, after G - A.B.C. &c again.
P.   How are the names of the notes distinguished?
M.   By the situation on Lines and Spaces.
P.   How many lines are made use of in Music?
M.   Five - the lowest called the 1st line, the next above the 2nd line &c counting upwards.
P.   Are there any more than five lines used in Music?
M.   Yes - the 1st additional line above the 5th line is call'd the 1st OVER LINE, the 2nd, the 2nd OVER LINE &c and the 1st additional line under the 1st line is call'd the 1st UNDER LINE, the 2nd, the 2nd UNDER LINE.'

All this dialogue has, of course, to be memorised and so the scene in the music room is one of quiet concentration, most girls working independently, but here and there an older girl helps one much younger and tests her knowledge. Meanwhile, the remaining student, away from the others, performs at the harpsichord with the master standing near by. Her copy is opened in Part Two - 'Progressive Lessons for Practice' - more than forty pages of short, graded pieces, many by Edward Miller himself, others, for example, by Lully, Bach, Handel, Rameau, and concluding with the well-known 'Air by Mr. Handel in Berenice.' Gavots and Minuets abound, together with the occasional Jigg, Ground or Larghetto, and there is even an Allegro composed by the King of Prussia! The young student, having played an 'Air with Variations' by Vanhall, to the satisfaction of her master, rejoins the group and another takes her place.

It would be interesting to know more of Miller's method. It seems unlikely that he would have time during the class lessons of the week to help every member individually at the harpsichord. Were some private lessons also necessary in order to complete the keyboard tuition? Neither would the master have much time in class for testing and noting the progress of each student's theoretical learning. Was some monitorial system employed whereby the older and more advanced students helped and supervised the younger pupils with their work? Unfortunately we are given no details, but 'Institutes of Music' appears to have been an immediate success, and in all probability, a 'best-seller' too. It was mentioned earlier in this chapter that the first impression was sold within a few days, that a second impression also appeared in 1783 and a fifth edition in 1785. By 1790 the thirteenth edition was being sold, and in 1805 the 'Doncaster, Nottingham and Lincoln Gazette' had an advertisement on April 12th for the 25th Edition. When originally published the sub-title to this work described it as 'Easy Instruction for the Harpsichord' but, by 1805 this had become 'For Young Beginners on the Pianoforte'. There were to be supplementary publications too. An 'Appendix to the Institutes' was promised for 1791 ('Twenty-four Exercises in all the Major and Minor Keys.' Op. 7) and, also in the same year, a 'Sequel to the Institutes'. ('Twelve Progressive Lessons for the Pianoforte or Harpsichord, with an accompaniment for the flute or violin.' Op. 8). A 'Musical Primer', described as a 'Companion to the Institutes' was advertised in the above periodical only two months before the author's death in 1807.

Few copies of the above would find their way into the late eighteenth-century free schools and public schools for boys, where music rarely figured in the curriculum. Some would be sold individually for use in private tuition, but the main demand would come from the private schools for girls, where some knowledge of music, together with the ability to play a keyboard instrument and perhaps sing a little, were regarded as most ladylike pursuits and socially useful accomplishments.

Some years before 'Institutes of Music' was first published the 'York Courant' of January 6th and 13th, 1778 had the following notice:

'MUSIC made EASY: or An entire new Method of learning to play on the HARPSICHORD, composed chiefly for the Use of young Ladies, and proper for Beginners on any Instrument; to which is added progressive Lessons for Practice.

By Edward Miller, Organist at Doncaster.
. . . . Price Five Shillings.'

This advertisement also asked prospective customers to order copies and pay for them as soon as possible so that the publishers would have some idea of the number required. A list of music dealers with whom orders could be placed was given, and the copies were promised for the following December.

Nothing further is known of this venture. 'Music Made Easy' does not appear to have materialised and no further reference can be found to it in the 'York Courant' or other periodical. Perhaps, after a disappointing response, the project was dropped for a while, but it is highly probable that after much re-thinking and considerable reconstruction, it finally achieved publication as 'Institutes of Music'. Both combined theoretical training with the playing of the harpsichord, and both appear to have been primarily intended for the use of young ladies. An interesting footnote to the above advertisement informs the reader that Miller's 'Elegies and Songs, composed for one or two voices', is now available in its Second edition. This, of course, refers to his 'Opera Three' dedicated to the Rev. Mr. Mason.

Chapter Seven

'Early in the morning, the weather being very favourable, persons of all ranks quitted their carriages with impatience and apprehension, lest they should not obtain seats, and presented themselves at the several doors of Westminster Abbey, which were advertised to be opened at Nine o'clock; but the door-keepers not having taken their posts . . . . . till near Ten o'clock, such a crowd of ladies and gentlemen were assembled together as became very formidable and terrific to each other, particularly the female part of the expectants; for some of these being in full dress, and every instant more and more incommoded and alarmed, by the violence of those who pressed forward, in order to get near the door, screamed; others fainted; and all were dismayed and apprehensive of fatal consequences: as many of the most violent, among the gentlemen, threatened to break open the doors; a measure, which if adopted, would, probably, have cost many of the most feeble and helpless their lives; as they must infallibly, have been thrown down, and trampled on, by the robust and impatient part of the crowd.

It was a considerable time after a small door at the west end was opened, before this press abated; as tickets could not be examined, and cheques given in return, fast enough, to diminish the candidates for admission, or their impatience.

However, except dishevelled hair, and torn garments, no real mischief seems to have happened. In less than an hour after the doors were opened, the whole area and galleries of the Abbey seemed too full for the admission of more company; and a considerable time before the performance began, the doors were all shut to every one but their Majesties, and their suite, who arrived soon after Twelve.'

Thus Charles Burney described the morning of Wednesday, May 26th 1784 when the first Handel Commemoration Concert was held. ('An Account of the Musical Performances in Westminster Abbey . . . . in . . . . 1784, in Commemoration of Handel', by Chas. Burney, Mus. Doc., F.R.S.) Within the Abbey, at the west end, a huge stage had been erected. This accommodated the organ, which was a new one built for Canterbury Cathedral, the two hundred and fifty members of the orchestra, all of whom had given their services, and the principal vocalists. Further staging at each side held a choir numbering more than two

THE HANDEL COMMEMORATION, 1784.
Choir and Orchestra in Westminster Abbey.
From an engraving in Charles Burney's 'Account'.

hundred and seventy. The King, Queen and the royal party viewed this vast array from the east end of the nave, where the royal box, upholstered in crimson velvet fringed with gold, had been built.

This event had been planned on an unprecedented scale and Burney also tells us that, 'in order to render the band as powerful and complete as possible, it was determined to employ every species of instrument that was capable of producing grand effects.' A pair of double-bass kettle drums were specially constructed, and two drums known as the 'Tower Drums', which had been captured by Marlborough at Malplaquet in 1709, were brought from the Tower of London. Six sackbuts, or trombones, were borrowed from the King's Band, and occupying a prominent position in the centre of the stage, was a double bassoon, about sixteen feet in length, which had been made for the coronation of George II but never used. Mr. Ashley of the Guards undertook to learn how to blow it. Behind the double bassoon was the harpsichord from which Mr. Joah Bates directed the proceedings, but not without help, for it was necessary to employ three assistant conductors in the more remote parts of the staging so that the five hundred and twenty five performers could all see the beat. Mr. Bates not only played the harpsichord but the organ too, for the keys of both instruments were connected by wires nineteen feet in length, a method of playing two instruments at once which, Burney says, was evolved by Handel. The more orthodox members of the orchestra were present in great numbers if unusual proportions. To the 48 first and 47 second violins were added 26 violas, 21 cellos and 15 double-basses. The drums, trombones and double bassoon have already been mentioned, and there were also 12 trumpets, 12 horns, 26 oboes, 26 bassoons, but only 6 flutes. Outstanding among the seventeen principal vocalists was Madame Mara. She had been a child prodigy on the violin but, when playing in London at the age of ten, some society ladies urged her to forsake the instrument as it was 'unfeminine'. This she did and turned instead to singing. We are told by 'Grove' (5th Edition) that, 'she had a voice remarkable for its extent and beauty, a great knowledge of music and a brilliant style of singing.' The concert began with the Coronation Anthem, 'Zadok the Priest', and ended with the chorus, 'The Lord shall reign for ever and ever', from 'Israel in Egypt'. Among the other items were the 'Dettingen Te Deum', the overtures from 'Esther' and 'Saul', and part of the anthem performed at the funeral of Her Majesty Queen Caroline. On the following evening, Thursday May 27th, the second concert took place at the Pantheon in Oxford Street. Burney tells us that the doors opened at six, the building was full at seven, and the concert began at eight with more than 1,600 people closely wedged together. He adds that the second concert was judiciously calculated to display Handel's abilities in dramatic and secular music, whilst the performances in the Abbey manifested in a wonderful manner his great powers as an ecclesiastical composer. An added attraction at the Pantheon was the appearance of Pacchierotti, the Italian male soprano. On the following Saturday, May 29th, a return to the Abbey was made for the third and what should have been the final concert, a performance of 'Messiah'. The Queen was so impressed by this that she asked for it to be repeated. Indeed, so general was the demand for more, that two further concerts were given in the Abbey. On Thursday morning, June 3rd, by the command of His Majesty, there was a fourth concert with a programme very similar to the first, and on Saturday morning, June 5th, by command of Her Majesty, 'Messiah' was heard again, at the fifth and final concert. The first Handel Commemoration was so successful that there was a strong desire for it to become an annual event. Tickets for the individual concerts were one guinea (£1.05p) each and total receipts were nearly £13,000. After paying expenses, £1,000 was granted to Westminster Infirmary and £6,000 to the Society of Musicians, which existed to care for 'Decayed musicians and their families'. Among the first members of this society, which was founded in 1738, were Handel, Boyce, Thomas Arne, Pepusch, Festing, Weideman and Dr. Maurice Greene. Handel bequeathed £1,000 to it and, in 1790, George III granted it a royal charter. Further Handel Commemorations took place in 1785, 1786 and 1787, and also in 1791 when Haydn was present.

The idea of holding this event came from three musical amateurs -the seventh Viscount Fitzwilliam, Sir Watkin Williams-Wynn who became Treasurer for the Commemoration, and Mr. Joah Bates. The seventh Viscount is best known today for the bequest to Cambridge University of his valuable collection of manuscripts, books, pictures and engravings, together with the interest on £100,000 for the building of a museum. Amongst his collection was a book of music for the virginals which had been given to him by Robert Bremner whose music shop was mentioned in chapter four. Bremner bought the book, now known as the Fitzwilliam Virginal Book, for ten guineas at the sale of Pepusch's effects in 1763. This branch of the Fitzwilliam family must not be confused with their distant relatives, the Fitzwilliams who have owned the Wentworth Woodhouse estates in Yorkshire since 1782, when the second Earl Fitzwilliam inherited them on the death of his uncle, the second Marquis of Rockingham. Mr. Joah Bates was Commissioner to the Victualling office and, since its inception in 1776, had been the Director of the Concerts of Ancient Music. This body, also known as the King's Concerts or Ancient Concerts, gave twelve concerts each year but only of music that was at least twenty years old, thus providing frequent opportunity for the worship of Handel. 'Messiah' was also performed annually. Bates was born in Halifax in 1741 and educated at Eton and King's College, Cambridge. Whilst at Cambridge he organised and conducted a performance of 'Messiah' in his native town, and this is believed to have been its first performance north of the Trent. On that occasion Herschel was a member of the orchestra.

The three approached the governors of the Musical Fund, that is, the Society of Musicians, who approved of the idea and promised to assist. Help also came from the Directors of the Concerts of Ancient Music who volunteered to manage and direct the celebration. The King promised his patronage and the Dean readily consented to the event being held in the Abbey. 1784 was regarded as a most appropriate year for the first Handel Commemoration, many people in this country believing it to be the centenary of the composer's birth, but due to the adoption of the Gregorian calendar by different countries at widely different times, it was only the ninety-ninth anniversary. Handel was born on February 23rd 1684/5.

During the preparations for this first commemoration Edward Miller introduced himself by publishing a pamphlet he had written on behalf of 'Professors of Music Residing in the Country'. This consisted of two letters, the first addressed to the Nobility and Gentry and also to the managers of the ensuing grand performance in Commemoration of Handel, and the second, written in similar vein, to the directors of the fund for the benefit of decayed musicians and their families living in London. Printed for George Wilkie at St. Paul's Churchyard, this pamphlet was priced sixpence, and the two letters were dated May 1st and 2nd 1784 respectively, a little more than three weeks before the commemoration began. The first letter referred to the forthcoming commemoration and observed that, as the performers were giving their services, a handsome profit should be made. It noted that the profits were to be used for charitable purposes, but the advertisements did not specify which particular charities were to benefit. The writer felt, therefore, that he could not miss the opportunity of appealing for help for country musicians:

'In London, the fund for decayed Musicians and their families, has long been established; but at present, Professors residing in the country are excluded from receiving any benefit from that fund, as it is confined to those only who reside in the metropolis, who, when sick, have a handsome weekly allowance, and, in the case of death, their widows relieved, and their children put out apprentices to some trade.'

The writer then urged that membership and benefits of the fund for decayed musicians and their families should be extended to include provincial musicians, and further suggested that if this were not possible, a new fund should be established for the purpose. He concluded - *'For myself I have nothing to ask. Going down the hill of life, I trust I shall have enough to last me to my journey's end. But happy, thrice happy shall I esteem myself, if it be my lot to procure comfort to the afflicted; to soften the bed of sorrow; or free from the iron hand of Oppression, the all-enduring and depressed soul of Genius.'*

Miller's timing was excellent. His appeal was launched at the most appropriate moment and could scarcely fail to be successful. The forthcoming commemoration had created a wide and increased interest in music and musicians, and some of the country musicians for whom Miller was pleading were freely giving their services, and would be playing in the Abbey and the Pantheon alongside their more fortunate London colleagues. Moreover, it was highly probable that a large sum would be raised for charitable purposes. The main problem was one of organisation. Should there be one fund embracing all musicians or a new musical fund for the country professors? 'The Yorkshire Journal and General Weekly Advertiser' of Saturday March 31st 1787 tells us what happened - 'We have the pleasure to inform our musical readers, that the benevolent plan of Dr. Miller, of this town, for a new Musical Fund, admitting country professors, has been adopted in London, under the patronage of his Majesty, who has granted the Opera House for a grand musical performance for the benefit of the Society to be conducted by Dr. Hayes of Oxford and Dr. Miller.' Notice of this concert appeared in the same paper a week later:

'NEW MUSICAL FUND

At the King's Theatre, in the Haymarket, London

On Thursday, April 12th 1787 will be

A GRAND CONCERT

Of Vocal and Instrumental Music

Consisting of upwards of Two Hundred Performers,

Under the direction of

DR. HAYES of Oxford and DR. MILLER of Doncaster,

First Violin by Mr. Cramer

For the benefit of THE NEW MUSICAL FUND'

Then followed full details of the programme, beginning with the overture to 'The Occasional Oratorio', ending with the Coronation Anthem, 'Zadok the Priest' and including a large number of miscellaneous items for voices, strings, woodwind and the grand pianoforte. A long review of this event appeared in the 'Yorkshire Journal' of April the 21st, the opening paragraph of which is given below:

'London, April 13th. OPERA HOUSE — NEW MUSICAL FUND
The idea for establishing a new musical fund for decayed musicians, admitting country professors, originated in a letter addressed by Dr. Miller, of Doncaster, to the directors of the commemoration of Handel, in the year 1784 - and the commencement last night was almost as auspicious as the old fund! The audience was such as it ought to be at a concert that was very fine of itself, and further refined by the application of the art to the purpose of beneficence.'

Almost a year later, on March 15th 1788, the 'Yorkshire Journal' announced another 'Grand Miscellaneous Concert' for the New Musical Fund, to be held in the King's Theatre, Haymarket on the evening of Thursday March 27th, commencing at seven o'clock. It was to be 'on the same grand scale as last year', with the added attraction of the 'celebrated Battle Piece' composed by Signor Raimondi. No report of this event can be found in subsequent issues of this paper, its next reference to the new fund being on May 9th 1789:

'On Saturday last the Rev. Dr. Willett, George Smart Esq., and Dr. Miller of this town waited on Lord Sydney with the address of the New Musical Fund, to his Majesty on his happy recovery. And on Monday Dr. Miller was appointed superintendent for the County of York, by the President and Committee of the said fund.'

Not many weeks later, on the night of June 17th, the King's Theatre, which had been designed by Vanbrugh, was burnt to the ground and during its rebuilding, its title and activities were transferred to the Pantheon, as the following notice from the 'Yorkshire Journal' of February 12th 1791 shows:

'KING'S THEATRE, PANTHEON
NEW MUSICAL FUND
Under the Patronage of their Royal Highnesses
THE PRINCE OF WALES and DUKE OF YORK
On Thursday, February 24th 1791
will be performed

A GRAND MISCELLANEOUS CONCERT
Of Vocal and Instrumental Music
For the benefit of the New Musical Fund
Established for the Relief of Decayed Musicians, their Widows,
and Orphans, residing in England.
Leader of the Band - MR. CRAMER.
Conductors - Dr. Hayes and Dr. Miller

— — — — — — — — — —

Pit and Boxes - 10s 6d (52½p)　　Galleries 5s. (25p)
The Doors will be open at Six o'clock, and the Performance begin at Seven.

— — — — — — — — — —

Such Ladies and Gentlemen as may be desirous of
encouraging the Society by subscribing to the Annual
Performance are respectfully informed that Tickets
(emblematical of the Institution, and which may be
retained by the Subscriber) are ready for delivery . . . . .'

One of these tickets is still in existence at the Headquarters of the
Royal Society of Musicians in Stratford Place, London. Engraved on
thick white paper, about seven inches by six, is an angelic figure seated
on a cloud and playing a lute. Below are the words:
'New Musical Fund, Established 1786.'

Doubtless the reader will have observed that recent references have
been not to 'Edward', but to 'Doctor' Miller. On June 24th 1786 the
'Cambridge Chronicle' reported that, 'Mr. Miller, Organist of
Doncaster, is expected to be admitted a Doctor of Music at the ensuing
Commencement, for which purpose he will keep a Music Act in Great St.
Mary's Church on Sunday the 2nd of July, wherein a considerable band
of performers both Vocal and Instrumental will be employed.' In the
issue of July 7th 1786 appeared the brief statement that, 'Dr. Edward
Miller, of Pembroke College, Organist of Doncaster, was created Doctor
of Music'. It is not known whether the manuscript in Cambridge University Library, of a Te Deum, Jubilate, Magnificat and Nunc Dimittis
in C, by Edward Miller is his Mus. Doc. exercise.

In the New Musical Fund concerts Miller's associate conductor was Dr. Philip Hayes who, after being organist at Worcester Cathedral, succeeded his father as Organist of Magdalen College, Oxford, and Professor of Music at the University. His sudden death in London was reported in the 'Doncaster Gazette' of March 25th 1797 - 'This gentleman lately came to town for the purpose of presiding over the concert for the benefit of the New Musical Fund. He dressed himself on Sunday morning in order to attend at the Chapel Royal, St. James, but was suddenly seized with the symptoms of dissolution and in a very short time expired.'

There are, in the British Library, two volumes of programmes of New Musical Fund concerts, with manuscript notes by Sir George T. Smart, the son of the George Smart mentioned earlier in this chapter. Sir George was a chorister and later organist of the Chapel Royal, and a noted conductor. He visited Beethoven in Vienna, and it was in his London home that Weber died. Though the two volumes contain many programmes of the Fund's annual concerts in the capital, most of the earlier ones are missing, the first to be included is that of 1794 and the next is for the year 1805.

A foreword to the 1794 programme gives reasons for the founding of the New Musical Fund and also states its aims:

'The preclusion of a great number of Musicians in London, and more particularly those residing in the Country, from being admitted Members of the Society under the patronage of His Majesty' - (that is, the Royal Society of Musicians) - 'has induced them to form themselves into a Society for the benefit of themselves, their wives and children, and in order to support a Fund for the aforesaid purposes, they intend to have an Annual Performance and propose to give two tickets to each Honorary Subscriber paying one guinea (£1.05p). The plan is, as soon as possible, to allow:

All widows left destitute £25 per annum, or make up to £25 p.a. whatever sum short of that their husbands leave them.

To put all orphans apprentices at the age of fourteen and to give them £10 as premium, and to allow two shillings (10p) per week for each child if their parents die before they arrive at that age. Temporary assistance to members in distress of ten to fifteen shillings a week'.

Next are details of the concert of 'Songs, Chorusses etc.' to be given on Thursday March 6th (1794) at the King's Theatre, Haymarket, and finally a list of subscribers' names is given, including that of 'Miller, Dr., Doncaster'. In the programme of 1805 Miller's name does not appear.

This was only two years before his death and he must have allowed his subscription to lapse, but, in the absence of intermediate programmes it is possible that he was still a subscriber in 1804.

The last programme included in the two volumes is that of 1841. For some unknown reason the New Musical Fund ceased to exist in the following year. It was not for lack of funds. 'The Times' estimated that it had, at the time of closure, between nine and ten thousand pounds, and this was shared amongst the professional members. There was no merger with the Royal Society of Musicians or any other body. After more than half a century of helping its members and their dependants it ceased to exist.

* * * * * *

One wonders whether Edward Miller attended the first Handel Commemoration Concerts described at the beginning of this chapter. He rarely tells us of his travels and engagements, and we have to seek this information from the columns of contemporary periodicals. On this occasion, however, when writing of something quite different, he gives a clue which suggests that he was in London at the time of the great event. In his 'History of Doncaster' (p. 158) he writes - 'Many years ago, in my way to London, I breakfasted at Biggleswade, and was told by the land-lord at the inn, that George Alexander Stevens was then in that town dangerously ill . . . . . I hastened to see my old friend . . . . . but ah! he was performing his last part! for death presently dropt the curtains!'

Stevens began his career on the stage at Norwich when Miller was a boy. He later performed more than once at the Old Theatre in Doncaster, where he again met Miller. He died on September 6th 1784 and the first Handel Commemoration Concert took place on May 26th of that year.

THE GRAND STAND.
From Miller's 'History of Doncaster'.

Chapter Eight

Now we must leave the grand concerts of the capital and its music funds too. The 'Yorkshire Journal', from which Miller's London successes have been quoted, tells also of his continuing activity in and around Doncaster - performing, teaching, composing and writing - thus giving a much more balanced picture of his life in the 1780's. There is no doubt that the commemoration concerts stimulated an interest in music throughout the country, particularly the music of Handel, and we see this reflected in the decision to hold a Festival of Music at Doncaster during the September (St. Leger) race-meeting of 1787, when the town, as usual, would be crowded with visitors. Advertisements on the first four Saturdays in September (ibid) announced a numerous chorus from Lancashire and Sheffield &c; instrumental performers from London, York, Durham and many provincial towns, with the local nobility including Earl Fitzwilliam, Lord Viscount Galway, Lord Viscount Downe and Sir George Cooke, Bart., acting as stewards. There were to be three morning concerts, 'Judas Maccabeus' on Wednesday September 26th, 'Messiah' on the 27th, and 'Acis and Galatea' on the 28th. Later 'The Occasional Oratorio' was substituted for 'Acis and Galatea'. The concerts were to be held in the parish (St. George's) church beginning 'precisely as the church clock strikes eleven'. The West Gallery was reserved for those who subscribed one and a half guineas for all three concerts, the middle isle *(sic)* for single ticket holders at half a guinea each, and elsewhere the seats cost five shillings. The principal vocalist was Madame Mara, and Dr. Miller conducted. Subsequent reports, on Sept. 29th and Oct. 6th (ibid), had nothing but praise for all concerned and particularly for Madame Mara who, at the 'Messiah' performance, 'indulged the audience with opening the oratorio - Comfort ye my people.' It is interesting to note that at the York Festival of 1823, Madame Catalini usurped 'Comfort ye' and 'Ev'ry Valley' from the tenor soloist in like manner. Did this arise from the determination of temperamental *prima donnas* to be first, or was it to satisfy an eager audience which would rather not wait until after the 'Pastoral Symphony' before hearing the internationally famous visitor? Many arias in 'Messiah' were exchanged between singers for single perform-ances even in Handel's day.

On the Sunday following the festival the Charity Sermon was preached in the parish church for the benefit of the Sunday schools. Madame Mara sang 'Pious Orgies' from 'Judas Maccabeus', some of the festival singers sang an anthem, 'Sing unto God, O ye Kingdoms', and the Sunday school children sang the hymn, 'Praise the Lord all ye that fear him'. The words of anthem and hymn were by the Vicar of Doncaster, the Rev. G. W. Hay Drummond, the music by Dr. Miller. The report of October 6th also states that Madame Mara, 'thinking the produce of the festival not adequate to Dr. Miller's trouble, generously returned him twenty guineas of her engagement, as did Mr. Meredith five guineas, nor would Mr. Warburton or Mr. Lawton accept of any gratuity'. There was a similar happening after the Sheffield Festival of 1788, when 'Messiah' and Handel's 'Joseph and his brethren' were performed in St. Paul's Church on the mornings of August 13th and 14th respectively, with Dr. Miller at the organ, and two concerts were held in the theatre on the same evenings. On August 23rd the 'Yorkshire Journal' reported that, 'the whole receipts amounted to £456-6-0 and notwithstanding Mr. Cramer returned ten guineas out of the fifty guineas he received, and Mrs. Billington, out of the eighty guineas she received, returned five, the expence *(sic)* attending such a number of performers is so great, that we are sorry to hear not more than forty pounds . . . . . . will be left for the charity.' (The Girls' Charity School, lately erected in Sheffield).

No doubt the disappointing financial results of these large under-takings, due to the heavy expenses or only moderate support, discouraged their frequent repetition. During the St. Leger race-meeting of 1788 there was only one concert (directed by Dr. Miller) together with the Charity Sermon on the Sunday, and in the following year there was no concert at all. There were, of course, other musical events occurring from time to time in which Edward was involved. In the August of 1789 for example, not long after the outbreak of revolution in France and the storming of the Bastille, immense preparations were taking place at Wentworth Woodhouse for the reception of the three royal brothers, the Prince of Wales and the Dukes of York and Clarence. Every exertion was being made to provide amusements for their entertainment and the 'Journal' reported on August 22nd that, 'a grand fete is to be exhibited on the second of September, for which cards are already sent out, the hour of meeting, nine in the evening; the best musical performers are to be engaged by Dr. Miller of this town, who is now composing music for this purpose, and is to conduct the performance.' Later in the same month, at one of the Doctor's concerts, the local people were able to hear this 'Ode and Song written in honour of his Royal Highness, the Prince of Wales on his visit to Wentworth House', (ibid, Sept. 26th 1789) and, in the following month Dr. Miller was again in demand, as this notice shows, (ibid, Oct. 17th 1789) when the Duke of Norfolk's Militia were in town:

'MANSION HOUSE, DONCASTER

In the Grand Room on Friday evening, October 23rd 1789

WILL BE

A BALL

With the Clarenets and French Horns of the Militia Band,
to accompany the Minuets.

Previous to the Ball some favourite Songs, Glees and Catches
will be performed by Miss Hitchcock, Messrs. Clifford,
Ryley, Nutter, etc.

Concerto on the Clarenet by Mr. Wright

Concerto on the Flute by Mr. Darcy

To be conducted by Dr. Miller

Tickets at 3s 6d each (17½p) . . . . . Begin at Seven o'clock'

The clarinet, or 'clarenet', as the paper spells it, was a relative new-comer to the orchestra and military band. Quite probably some who attended the above event would neither have seen nor heard one before.

From Miller the performer, we turn to Miller the author, much occupied, no doubt, by writing and research during the 1780's. Chapter Six told of his Opera Four, 'Institutes of Music', first appearing in 1783, and Opera Five, also printed by Longman and Broderip, was being advertised as 'just published' in the 'Yorkshire Journal' of April 28th and May 12th 1787. This was his 'Elements of Thorough Bass and Composition', the lengthy sub-title of which sums up the purpose of the book's eighty-eight pages: 'In which the Rules of Accompaniment for the Harpsichord and Piano Forte are rendered amusing by the Intro-duction of Eight Italian, Eight French and Twelve English Songs collected from the Works of eminent composers Antient and Modern, with Proper Lessons for Practice. Written by way of conversation between the Master and his Pupil for the use of such performers as are unacquainted with the principles of Harmony.' The book priced one guinea (£1.05p), was most humbly dedicated to Lord Viscount Galway, K.B., whose country seat, Serlby Hall, Nottinghamshire, was about fourteen miles from Doncaster. Miller appears to have been very friendly with Lord Galway and his first wife, for when writing of Serlby in his 'History of Doncaster', (p. 306) he remarks that, 'here many of the happiest days of my life were spent.' He also named one of his psalm-tunes 'Gallway' which, as 'Galway', the modern form of spelling, is found today in 'Hymns, Ancient and

Modern, Revised'. Early in the following year, on January 5th 1788, the 'Journal' announced the forthcoming publication of Opera Six, consisting of an anthem in score, with instrumental parts separately printed, and a hymn, 'as sung by the Children of the Sunday Schools at Doncaster'. Both anthem and hymn were also adapted for single voice and harpsichord. The reader will realize from their titles - 'Sing unto God, O ye Kingdoms', and 'Praise the Lord all ye that fear Him' - that these were the two items composed for the Charity Sermon of the previous September. The same advertisement told of proposals for printing by subscription Miller's arrangements of Corelli's Trio Sonatas, Opus One and Two. Six Sonatas from Opus One were to be arranged for the organ and six from Opus Two for harpsichord and pianoforte. These twelve arrangements, in one volume, were announced as 'just published' in the 'Yorkshire Journal' of June 27th 1789, as were the 'Anthem and Hymn' of Opera Six. Later Corelli's Opus Three and Four were treated similarly. Being arrangements, Miller did not give an Opera number to the Corelli, neither was such a number given to his next work which was published in 1790 and to which Chapter Ten will be chiefly devoted. The 'Yorkshire Journal' of July 31st 1790 tells us that, 'Dr. Miller of this town has just received a letter from Frederick Nicolai Esq., informing him that his Majesty has graciously permitted his name to be put at the head of Dr. Miller's list of subscribers to his proposed Publication of Psalms for the use of Parish Churches.'

Finally we must remember Edward's non-musical activities, though evidence is scanty and dates scarce. Enough can be gleaned, however, from records and periodicals to indicate that, as the eighteenth century progressed, he acquired a variety of business interests. In the 1780's he was still occupying the 64 acres on the Carr, for he relates in his 'History of Doncaster' that he had this land until the expiration of the lease in 1793 (See Chapter 5). He also tells of buying a further 20 acres and selling at a very substantial profit but gives no dates for this. The house he built there, Carr Grange, was his property until about the end of the century when he sold it to Thomas Copley of Nether Hall, who was mentioned briefly at the end of Chapter Four. There was evidence in Chapter Three of his interest in the letting and sub-letting of small properties, and an advertisement in the 'York Courant' of April 2nd 1782 is a further illustration of this activity:

'TO PIPE MAKERS, DONCASTER

Whereas a Pipe Maker is much wanted, there not being one in the Town, Any sober industrious Man will meet with good Encouragement and may enter immediately into the House lately occupied by Samuel Lumley. There is a Pot, Furnace, Mold, Grates, and everything necessary on the Premises for the Business, which will be sold at a fair valuation.

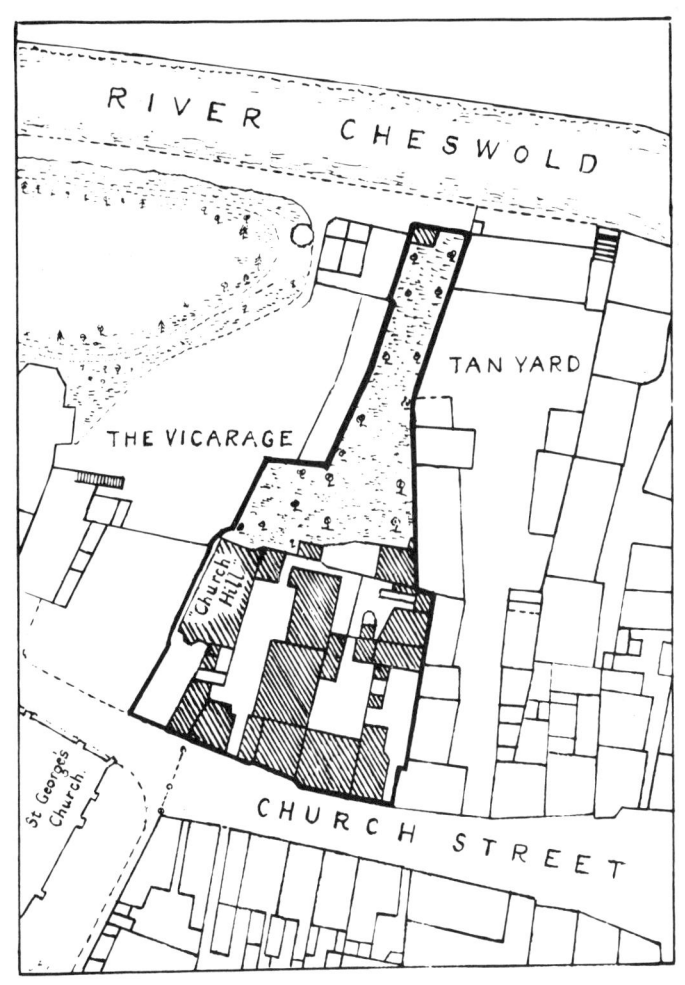

A PLAN OF THE MILLER PROPERTY.
('Church Hill', Miller's Yard and Church Street).

Rent of house and premises 5 gns. a year. Inquire of Mr. Miller, Doncaster.
Letters (Post Paid) will be answered. This will be no more advertised.'

In 1972 the land on both sides of Church Street, immediately to the
east of 'Church Hill,' which included the site of Miller's Yard and its
surrounding buildings, was excavated by the Department of the Environ-
ment and Doncaster Museum, under the direction of Mr. M. J. Dolby,
Keeper of Antiquities at the Museum. This resulted in the unearthing of
part of the walls of the Roman fort and a Roman building. Also, quite
near to Miller's house, a mass of broken clay pipes was found together
with the remains of a pipe-making kiln. Some of the pipe-stems, now in
Doncaster Museum, are impressed, 'S. LUMLEY'. The first-known
mention of Church Street is in 1796. Before that time it was, with neighbouring streets, regarded as part of Fishergate. (See p. 17).

(Doncaster Archives, Judicial 5e) also for 1782, show two affidavits
sworn by Edward Miller, the first on March 26th, alleging that Thomas
Watson, innkeeper of Doncaster owed him £12 and upwards, this being
two years' rent for the use of a close of land and premises. Thomas
Watson kept the White Lion Inn which at that time was in French Gate.
The second affidavit, dated May 6th, states that Thomas Timms,
Yeoman, owed Miller £12 ,, 3 ,, 9 (£12.19) for the use and occupation of
certain closes of land and premises, together with £5,,5,,0 due on a
promissory note. Unfortunately the situation of the above land and
premises is not known, neither do we know whether the property was
Edward's or whether he held it on lease, but these affidavits provide
further evidence of his continued interest in land and property trans-
actions which, no doubt, augmented his income from music. Some time
before the end of the century he became the owner of sandpits in
Wheatley. He mentions, 'my estate in the Sand Closes in Wheatley' in his
Last Will and Testament. An old day-book of the firm of Thomas
Anelay, the Doncaster builders, tells of 41 loads of sand being supplied
to them from Dr. Miller's sand pits at Wheatley between March 1798 and
May 1800. Hatfield, in his 'Historical Notices of Doncaster', (Vol.3, p.
81. 1870) talking of what is now known as Wheatley Lane, says:

'In the recollection of many, not a dwelling of any description was
to be seen in the road except the house near the sand pits built by Dr.
Miller.'

Edward also, at some time unknown, had land on Town Fields and
built a small house there. The evidence for this is found in the 'Doncaster
Gazette' of April 19th 1861 -

'In the past week Mr. W. H. Forman acquired 22 acres of land on Town Field in close contiguity to the borough, the property of Mr. John Warrington. The cottage, now used as a farm house, originally built by the late Dr. Miller, of eminent musical celebrity and author of the 'History of Doncaster', is, together with the homestead, included in the purchase.'

Our final example is much more precise, for the exact position of the property is known. The 'Doncaster Courtiers' (Vol. 4, p. 247) of July 26th 1804 has this entry:

'One other conveyance in Consideration of Two hundred and Sixty two pounds, to Dr. Miller, his Heirs and Assigns, three Cottage Houses in Fishergate, Doncaster with the Buildings and Yards in the Occupation of Ann Hall, Thomas Darley and William Travis. Also two Cottage Houses there with the Yards thereto belonging in the Occupations of Mrs. Brailsford and John Pickman with the Land Tax and Appurtenances.'

The Water Rents Book of 1797 shows that the above tenants all dwelt in High Fishergate, a street to the east of the church, which ran from the Market Place in the direction of the river. At that time, 'Mrs.' or 'Mistress' was a common courtesy title and did not necessarily imply matrimony. Most probably the Mrs. Brailsford mentioned as a tenant was the Elizabeth, mother of Edward's two natural sons.

For the Miller family the year 1785 marked the beginning of a period of tragedy. In that year his son Thomas, the second of his children to bear that name, was drowned at the age of fifteen while serving as a midshipman on the East Indiaman 'Halsewell'. Not long before he was drowned, perhaps on his last visit to his home, Thomas and another person scratched their names on one of the small panes of glass in a bedroom window at 'Church Hill.' These are still to be seen there -

Thos Miller
John Wilment
1785

Nothing is known of John Wilment - perhaps he was one of Thomas's seagoing companions.

In the following year, 1786, Elizabeth, the eldest daughter, died at the age of 22, and the years 1791 and 1792 saw the deaths of the two remaining daughters, Mary aged 22 and Lois aged 20, leaving only one surviving legitimate child, William Edward. At her death in 1791 Mary had been married for less than a year to her cousin, William Richard Beckford Miller, the son of Edward's brother Thomas, the Bungay bookseller. This William (1769-1844), after working for a publisher, started business on his own account at 5, Old Bond Street, London in 1790, his first publication being his uncle Edward's 'Psalms of David'. One would like to think that his uncle changed his publisher on this occasion in order to help William, his nephew and son-in-law, and Mary, his daughter, at the start of their married life and new business venture. Unfortunately Mary lived only long enough to see her father's 'Psalms of David' successfully launched and in great demand.

'Church Hill' looking West, with portion of Roman fort wall in the immediate foreground, on the site of Miller's Yard. (Photograph, 'Doncaster Evening Post').

Chapter Nine

Let us for a while return to the England of two centuries ago, when the third George had completed the first quarter of his long reign and the population of England and Wales was less than eight million; when coal, iron and steam were beginning to change the face of the country and the American colonies were slipping quickly from our grasp; when the British workman toiled the clock round for two or three shillings a day and his unschooled children often joined him in coal-pit or factory at the tender age of eight or nine; when land enclosure was proceeding apace and Edward Miller's horses were sinking into the morass on Potteric Carr as he tried to tame his recently acquired acres.

It is Sunday, and the worshippers, summoned by bells, walk the well-trodden paths to the village church and take their places in the high-sided box pews that fill the nave. Each pew has its door, and when the occupants are seated, they see little of their surroundings save for the rafters above and the upper-works of the lofty three-decker pulpit. A screen separates nave from chancel, and the latter, apart from the altar and some memorial slabs, is quite bare and without seats or stalls. From the gallery at the west end of the building come sounds of fiddle, flute and bassoon as the village musicians prepare their instruments and thumb through the music to find the day's metrical psalms. With them are more people of the village, unselected and untrained, but charitably known as 'the singers'. The Lord and Lady of the Manor, with children and attendants, arriving a few minutes late, walk up the aisle to the bowing and curtseying of the congregation and enter their curtained and canopied pew. Mattins can now begin.

Much of the service appears to be a duet between parson and clerk, for the latter dominates responses and prayers, leaving the humble villagers to follow him meekly in undertones. There is more congregational involvement, however, immediately before and after the sermon when the metrical psalms are sung. Unfortunately the singing is a slow and laborious process, for many are unable to read, and the practice of 'lining out' is adopted. The first line is read aloud by priest or clerk and immediately sung by the congregation led by the players and singers in the gallery. The next line is similarly treated, this saying and singing continuing until all the verses of the psalm are completed. The speed, or rather lack of speed of the singing, makes this slow process even slower, and throughout, the congregation stands and turns round to face the gallery musicians.

(The practice of 'lining out' was suggested by a Parliamentary Ordnance of 1644 as a temporary measure to help non-readers. It had not completely disappeared two centuries later!)

Leaving this church we visit another, a much more imposing building in a large town. This too has a gallery at the west end, but we see no rural orchestra seated therein, the space being occupied instead by an organ, a somewhat uncommon feature for a parish church of the 1770's. (Before the nineteenth century only a few parish churches possessed organs. Church choirs and choirmasters as we understand them, were unknown.) Surely, with such an imposing instrument, near which a body of singers group themselves, and an accomplished organist, the music must be of a much higher standard! As we listen, however, we find to our dismay that the singing is even slower and more laboured than before, for in addition to the 'lining out' and the slow tempo, the organist indulges in another custom of the period, introducing shakes at the end of each line and interludes between the verses. Moreover he plays much too loudly and the singers' faces redden, the veins in their necks stand out as they try in vain to compete.

(Congregational singing in our parish churches was, until the nineteenth century, almost wholly confined to metrical versions of the psalms. 'Human hymns', as Scholes describes them, were not, on doctrinal grounds, permissible. The metrical psalms sung at the beginning and end of the service, or perhaps before and after the sermon, were additional to the psalms set for the day which, in our parish churches were read from the prayer book, and in cathedrals and collegiate foundations were sung to chants.)

On returning to the present day we may find the reader wondering whether the above pictures of the past are typical of the services in our parish churches of two hundred years ago, and to answer this we must turn to the literature of the mid-seventeenth to mid-nineteenth centuries, remembering that our concern is not with the music of cathedrals and other special places but only with that of the numerous parish churches in the towns and villages of an England before the Industrial Revolution. Neither must we forget that some churches had no music at all. Instrumentalists of sufficient accomplishment were not to be found in every parish, organs were generally too expensive to acquire, harmoniums and American organs were as yet unknown, and barrel organs, which later became so popular and could be operated by non-musicians, were still in their infancy. It is not surprising, therefore, to find that many writers from the Restoration onwards present a depressing picture of the standard of worship in our parish churches, much of the blame being laid at the feet of the parish clerks who controlled an important part of each service and were immediately responsible for whatever music there was. The term 'clerk' was originally applied to men in holy orders but later it was given to the important lay functionary in each parish who led the responses, pronounced the 'Amens' at the end of prayers and sermons, selected, announced and perhaps 'lined out' the metrical psalms, and if required to do so, gave the note for singing on his adjustable pitch-pipe. The clerk also had other duties including the keeping of the church registers. The Parish Clerks of London are one of the City Livery Companies, being incorporated in the year 1232. Their Charter stated that, 'Every person that is chosen Clerk of a Parish shall first give sufficient proof of his abilities to sing at least the tunes which are used in parish churches,' but, by the mid-eighteenth century, this test was no longer applied. Probably the parish clerks of London were among the most proficient, for they had their own hall, which possessed an organ, where they could learn how to set and sing the psalms, but even they suffered severely during the Commonwealth. John Playford, who was a clerk himself, said in the preface to his book, 'Psalms and Hymns in Solemn Musick of Foure Parts', published in 1671 - 'At this day the Best, and almost all the Choice Tunes are lost, and out of use in our Churches, nor must we expect it otherwayse, when in and about this Great City, in over One Hundred Parishes, there is but few Parish Clerks to be found that have either Ear and Understanding to Set one of these Tunes Musically as it ought to be.' The clerks, therefore, had to begin again to learn their duties, and whilst those in and around London could meet regularly for this purpose, the great majority probably received no help at all. More than a century later, on Sunday, August 14th 1791 Parson Woodforde wrote - 'There was a large Congregation at Church. Poor old Js. Smith, my clerk, made a shocking hand of it in singing this Afternoon ......much laughed at.' ('The Diary of a Country Parson'). Charles Burney had suggested a remedy for this about a decade earlier in the third volume of his 'History of Music' - 'The greatest blessing to lovers of music in a parish church is to have an organ in it sufficiently powerful to render the voices of the Clerk, and of those who join in his outcry, wholly inaudible. Indeed, all the reverence for the psalms seems to be lost by the wretched manner in which they are usually sung.' Fortunately for the ear-drums of numerous congregations a much quieter method of silencing parish clerks was finally adopted, an Act of Parliament of 1844 divesting them of most of their duties. Even then some of them were loath to depart and lingered on well after the middle of the century. The Rev. R. W. Hiley, who became Vicar of Wighill, near Tadcaster, in 1863, tells in his book, 'Memoirs of half a century', of his clerk leaving his desk during the services and explaining afterwards: 'I hear 'em going on all wrong, so I taks a turn down the church and sets 'em all right.'

In his 'History of Doncaster' (p. 88), Edward Miller tells us what happened in his own church - 'The psalmody in this church till the year 1790, was conducted upon the same plan as that of other parochial churches in this kingdom: where the parish clerk had the choice both of the words of a psalm, and the tune to be sung. His custom was to send the organist not the *words,* but only the *name* of the tune, and how often it was to be repeated. Strange absurdity! How could the organist, placed in this degrading situation, properly perform his part of the church service? Not knowing the words, it was impossible for him to accommodate his music to the various sentiments contained in different stanzas; consequently, *his* must be a mere random performance, and frequently producing improper effects.'

When we recall that Edward became organist at Doncaster in 1756, we realize that he must have suffered this 'degrading situation' for at least thirty-four years! Little is known of the parish clerks who officiated during the half century that he was organist, except for an entry in the Vestry Book for 1770 - 'Mr. Senior, Clerk of the Church, had a black gown of Bombazine on Whit Sunday or thereabouts, which never clerk had before' - and a notice in the 'Yorkshire Gazette' of February 28th 1795, telling of the death of John Butler, aged 63, Clerk for 'near 20 years.'

The church musicians often presented problems too, refusing to co-operate with priest or clerk, resenting help or advice, and objecting to congregational participation, though frequently their own efforts left much to be desired. In the 'Oxford Companion to Music' (Scholes) we read the following account given by a Suffolk clergyman in 1764: 'The Performers are placed in a Single Seat, sometimes a raised seat like a stage. Here they form themselves into a round Ring, with their Faces to each other and their Backs to ye Congregation. Here they murder Anthems, chuse improper Psalms, leave off in ye middle of a sentence, sing Psalms of all kinds to new, jiggish Tunes. If ye Minister offers to direct Them, "He may mind his Text; he may sing himself; they will sing as they list or not at all." They frequently leave their own Parish Church and go in a Body to display their Talents in other Churches. I have known them stroll six or seven miles for this purpose, sometimes with a young female singer or two in their train'. We learn from 'The Mirror of Music' (Scholes) that such visiting 'musickers' did not always deem it necessary to inform the incumbent that they wished to visit his church. They just arrived, walked in and made for the gallery and, after tuning their instruments, handed a piece of paper to the clerk which told him what hymns or anthem were to be sung. Parson Woodforde experienced trouble with his 'singers' too. After asking, on more than one occasion, his Castle Cary singers to say the responses during the Communion Service, and not to sing them, they were all 'highly affronted' and stayed away on the following Sunday. (Diary, November, 1769).

ST. GEORGE'S CHURCH, DONCASTER, BEFORE 1853.

From the North of England a record of 1770 gives the following picture of the music in the parish church (now the Cathedral) of Sheffield - 'Before the west window, high over the gallery, was a kind of immense large box hung in chains, into which, by the aid of a ladder, musicians and singers, male and female, contrived to scramble, and with the aid of bum basses, hautboys, fiddles, and various other instruments, accompanying shrill and stentorian voices, they contrived to make as loud a noise as heart could wish'. This quotation does not mention the congregation, perhaps because the majority of its members took no part in the singing. In his 'Thoughts on the present performance of Psalmody' (1791) Dr. Miller says - 'If any one should step into a parish church while the psalm is singing, would he not find the greater part of the congregation totally inattentive? Irreverently sitting - talking to each other - taking snuff - winding up their watches, or adjusting their apparel? and must he not think they entered the house of God from mere form and custom? Impelled by no religious motives, and so ignorant as not to know that it is as much their duty to join the clerk in singing the psalms, as it is their duty to join the minister in reading the psalms.' Thomas Hardy, whose father and grandfather were both church musicians, tells us in 'Under the Greenwood Tree' that his account of Mellstock Choir and its gallery musicians was intended to be a true picture at first hand of the early nineteenth century. We join the service at Mellstock on the Christmas morning when something happened which, 'had never happened before within the memory of man.' During the singing feminine voices coming from the schoolgirls' aisle were, 'as mighty as those of the regular singers'. There was much whispering in the gallery once the sermon had begun -

'Brazen faced hussies!' said Bowman . . . . .

'Tis the gallery have got to sing, all the world knows,' said Mr. Penny, (the boot and shoe maker). 'Why, souls, what's the use o' the ancients spending scores of pounds to build galleries if people down in the lowest depths of the church sing like that at a moment's notice?' . . . . .

'When all's said and done, my sonnies,' Reuben (the tranter) said, 'there'd have been no real harm in their singing if they had let nobody hear 'em, and only jined in now and then.'

At different times attempts were made to improve the services, particularly those parts in which the congregation joined, and the employment of an itinerant singing master was one method adopted. Early in the eighteenth century Joseph Addison, who was the son of a parson who became Dean of Lichfield, wrote the following in the 'Spectator' concerning Sir Roger de Coverley - 'At his coming to his Estate he found his Parishioners very irregular; and that in order to make them kneel and join in the Responses, he gave every one of them a Hassock and a Common-prayer Book; and at the same Time employed an itinerant Singing-Master, who goes about the Country for that Purpose, to insruct them rightly in the Tunes of the Psalms; upon which they now very much value themselves, and indeed out-do most of the Country Churches that I have ever heard.' (No. 112. Monday, July 9th 1711). In his pamphlet, 'Thoughts on the present performance of Psalmody' (1791), Dr. Miller advocated the employment of an itinerant Singing Master in any parish which had no organ and therefore no organist to undertake the training of the young people and interested adults. Unfortunately, not all parishes had a 'Sir Roger' willing to pay for such instruction, and not all Singing Masters were so successful. In a charge to the clergy in 1790 Beilby Porteus, Bishop of London, complains of the monopolising of the psalmody in the country parishes by a 'select band of singers who have been taught by some itinerant master to sing in the worst manner a most wretched set of psalm tunes in three or four parts.' ('Oxford Companion to Music', Scholes. p. 34).

For some years before Bishop Porteus made this complaint, a quite different approach to the problem was being tried in certain town and city churches which had organs and organists, and which were regularly attended by Sunday School children. Robert Raikes, though not the first person to start a Sunday School, was one of the founders of the movement and the idea spread rapidly after he had written an anonymous account of some early Sunday Schools in his paper, 'The Gloucester Journal', in 1783. A year later John Wesley remarked in his own journal that he found such schools springing up everywhere he went, and by 1795, the London Society for the Establishment of Sunday Schools had 65,000 scholars. Children who attended church and school on Sundays for secular and religious instruction, together with those in attendance at the relatively few weekday schools for the poor which existed in the eighteenth century, were generally known as 'charity children'. Many thousands of London charity children met annually in St. Paul's Cathedral to form a choir, greatly impressing Haydn in 1792 and Berlioz in 1851. In 1858 and 1859 there were similar performances in the Crystal Palace with choirs of more than four thousand children. With the coming of such children to the Sunday services and the appointment of more organists as more organs were introduced, an entirely new situation was created, particularly in towns. In addition to the clerk, perhaps untrained, and the gallery singers and players, frequently a law unto themselves, the capable organist now appeared, often desirous of improving the music of the services and seeing in the Sunday School children a means of so doing. On July 14th 1787 the following account appeared in the 'Yorkshire Journal' - 'To the credit of Dr. Miller, the organist of this town, he has undertaken to teach, by the ear only, some of the boys belonging to the Sunday Schools to join (or perhaps, more properly, to lead) the congregation in the singing of psalms, agreeable to the plan recommended by Dr. Vincent (an abstract of which was given in our last week's paper); and we hope to find this part of divine service rendered at once delightful and entertaining by the whole congregation joining therein. It would be of great use, if such as wish to render their assistance in promoting this desirable end, would sometimes give their attendance on the evenings when the boys practise; by such attendance the tunes would become familiar to the ear, and, by a little practice, the modulation of every voice might be brought to that pitch which would make the whole harmonious, and give such of the female part of the congregation as wish to join in this delightful part of divine service, an opportunity of assisting in the general harmony, without the pain of having their sweet notes entirely lost between the over-strained voice of a few individuals (whose motives for singing may be good ones but for want of judgement much misapplied) and the loud roar of a full toned organ.' Dr. Vincent, Rector of All Hallows the Great and Less, London, had recently published a treatise on 'The Singing of Psalms' in which he deplored the low standard of parochial music in many churches. His remedy was to train Sunday School children 'to perform the musical part of the service with sufficient accuracy to attract and delight', thus helping, 'the whole body of the people to perform their part.' He criticised the organ playing of the period as generally too loud, and called for the abolition of the select bands of gallery singers.

The first Sunday Schools to be established in Doncaster were only a few months old when the above article appeared. The 'Yorkshire Journal' of October 21st 1786 reported that on the previous Sunday, the vicar, the Rev. Mr. Drummond had preached a sermon in favour of instituting such schools in the town, and the issue of November 4th gave accounts of two meetings held on the previous Wednesday and Thursday, the 1st and 2nd of November. The first was a gathering of gentlemen, clergy and inhabitants in the chancel of the parish church at which it was resolved that Sunday Schools should be immediately established, and at the second, a meeting of the Corporation, it was agreed to give fifty pounds as an annual donation towards their support. ('Doncaster Courtiers.' Vol. 4, p. 176). A week later the same paper told of a meeting of the Free and Accepted Masons held in the Town Hall on Wednesday November 8th, at which the Worshipful Master, Dr. Miller, spoke in favour of Sunday Schools being opened in Doncaster and it was agreed to donate five guineas towards this 'laudable charity'. Events thereafter moved quickly for the 'Y.J.' of December 23rd said that two Sunday Schools for boys and two for girls had been opened in the town, and a fortnight later on January 6th 1787 it informed its readers of 120 boys and 154 girls being brought to church on the previous Sunday.

It is interesting to consider whether Edward taught small groups of boys to help the congregation in the singing of psalms or whether the group included girls also. The 'Yorkshire Journal' recently quoted, (July 14th 1787) used the word 'boys' but elsewhere the word 'children' is generally found. In his 'History of Doncaster' (p. 89, 1804), Miller wrote - 'Eight children, with good voices, are taught by the organist or his deputy, who attend one evening in the week for that purpose. These children are paid by the parish, and their voices, united with the organ, prove a sufficient guide to the rest of the congregation.' This was the outcome of a decision taken about six years earlier, as the Vestry Minutes for June 18th 1798 show -

'Resolved . . . . . . that the sum of ten guineas a year be paid quarterly . . . . . . to Dr. Miller to be laid out in providing a proper person to attend at the church on Friday evenings to teach the children to sing the church service, and to a person to blow the organ bellows . . . . . . and to eight children to attend the church service to sing under the direction of Dr. Miller . . . . . .'

Whether the training was confined to boys only as the 'Yorkshire Journal' states, is very doubtful, for in 'Thoughts on the present performance of Psalmody' (1791) Miller urges that the masters *and mistresses* of the Sunday and other charity schools should attend with their children to be instructed. The Doctor certainly included girls' voices on special occasions. In the last chapter mention was made of the Charity Sermon which ended the 'Leger' week of 1787 and at which some of the scholars performed a hymn specially written by Dr. Miller for the occasion, a hymn which was subsequently published. The 'Yorkshire Journal' of October 6th printed the words of this hymn and later in the same year, on December 22nd, printed a hymn for Christmas Day, also to be sung in the church by children of the Sunday School. There are directions on both hymns, different verses being marked 'Chorus; Semi-Chorus; Two girls; Two boys; Girl's Solo and Boy's Solo.' Reporting the latter event the 'Doncaster Journal' of December 29th 1787 said - 'A select number of children educated at the Sunday Schools in this town, having been instructed by Dr. Miller to accompany the organ in the singing psalms, on Christmas Day gave the congregation much satisfaction in the performance of the occasional hymn . . . . . . a convincing proof of how soon some degree of perfection may be attained in singing, without any other knowledge in music than that acquired by the ear, under the direction of a judicious instructor.'

From these humble beginnings we see how the modern parish church choir gradually developed, when in December 1817, ten years after Edward's death, the Doncaster Vestry meeting resolved -

'That Mr. Wragg shall be engaged to teach the singers and to attend the singing himself at an annual salary of twenty guineas . . . . . . that two men singers be engaged to assist in the singing at a salary of three guineas each (£3.15), and also that a number of children be selected and engaged to assist in the singing at a salary of one guinea each, number not to exceed twenty.' Mr. Wragg was a music dealer and teacher with a shop in Frenchgate.

Edward was one of the first to realize that children of the Sunday School could be successfully employed to teach the words and music of the metrical psalms to their often uneducated elders, thus greatly increasing congregational involvement in the services. He pioneered this method, not only by example, but also by advocating its use in his 'Psalms of David' (1790) and his 'Thoughts on the present performance of Psalmody' (1791). The fact that the training of the Sunday School children was often the work of an organist, and the organ itself was a help to the congregation, led to the gradual introduction of more and more organs to churches. This marked the beginning of the end of the gallery musicians, and of the clerk as an important functionary in the service. 'Lining out' came to end also.

In this chapter we have met clerics, clerks and congregations; church musicians and charity children; gallery singers and itinerant singing masters - but little mention has been made of the actual music with which all were concerned. The metrical psalms themselves were also in need of reform, and the story of the changes effected, in which Edward again played a prominent part, requires at least one chapter to itself.

That the children, after admiffion, fhall be fubject to the following regulations, a copy of which to be hung up in the fchools : That from the firft *Sunday* in *March* to the laft in *October*, they fhall attend their refpective fchools at eight o'clock in the morning ; that thofe who are able to ufe a com mon prayer book fhall find the proper pfalms and collects for the day , fhall read the " directions for behaviour in the different parts of public worfhip" (which are bound up with their prayer books), the epiftle, gofpel, pfalms, and fecond leffon ; and the lower claffes of children fhall read a portion in the eafier books provided for them ; that they fhall all, with their teachers, go in order, two and two, to church, and fhall then re turn in like order to their fchools, and be fent home till two o'clock, when they fhall go again to fchool, and read one or more of the evening pfalms or leffons, till public fervice, which they and their teachers fhall attend as before ; after which they fhall return to fchool in like order, and continue till fix o'clock repeating their *church catechifm*, and being inftructed in whatever *explanation* of it is approved of by the committee, and be then difmiffed.

Extract from a copy of the Sunday School Regulations, Doncaster.

Chapter Ten

Thomas Sternhold was Groom of the Robes to His Majesty King Henry VIII and received a legacy when his royal master died. It is most likely that he occupied a similar position under King Edward VI, and from about 1545 to 1547 he served as Member of Parliament for Plymouth. He was interested too in 'hymn' writing, a subject which had been greatly stimulated after the Reformation by the development of printing and the increasing use of the vernacular. As early as 1501 a book of hymns had been published in Bohemia, and in 1524 Luther's first hymn-book appeared. Thomas Sternhold's contribution was to paraphrase some of Miles Coverdale's translations of the Psalms of David using a popular ballad metre of the day. His singing of these metrical psalms attracted attention and Edward VI encouraged him to publish his work. The resultant volume, dedicated to the king and containing nineteen metrical psalms, was published with the title of, 'Certayne Psalmes, chosen out of the Psalter of David and drawen into English metre, by Thomas Sternhold, grome of ye Kynge's Maiesties roobes.' A larger volume containing thirty-seven of his paraphrases appeared shortly after his death in 1549, and in 1551 seven more were added, making a collection of forty-four. The additional seven, however, were not by Sternhold but attributed to John Hopkins, a Suffolk clergyman and schoolmaster. There was no music in the above books.

In 1553 Edward VI died and the Catholic Mary Tudor became Queen. Many English and Scottish divines fled to Geneva, the home of Calvinism, to escape the persecution which followed, taking the metrical psalms of Sternhold and Hopkins with them. There they found a French metrical psalter of eighty-three psalms in use, each with its own tune, and there were metrical versions also of the Ten Commandments and Nunc Dimittis.

As in this country, the French sang metrical psalms but not 'human hymns', believing that only what had biblical authority should be used in public worship. The music of this French psalter was of a high standard and profoundly influenced the next English version, which was the 'One and Fiftie Psalmes of David in Englishe metre', printed in Geneva in 1556. The forty-four paraphrases of Sternhold and Hopkins had grown to fifty-one by the addition of seven written by William Whittingham, afterwards Dean of Durham, and each of the fifty-one, together with the metrical version of the Ten Commandments which was included in an Appendix, had its own tune. In no subsequent psalter was there a different tune for each psalm.

On the death of Mary in 1558 Elizabeth became Queen and the English psalter came home again. A year later, the legality of metrical psalm singing was upheld and thereafter it had a recognised place in the morning and evening services. The years 1558 and 1560 saw further editions of the psalter, and in 1561 two more were published, one in London and the other in Geneva. More paraphrases were added, the Appendix grew in size, new tunes appeared and old tunes disappeared. Very few of the tunes of 1556 survived these constant revisions. In both the editions of 1561 the tune now known as the 'Old Hundredth' and the words we associate with it - 'All people that on earth do dwell' - came together for the first time.

In 1562 John Day, the printer 'dwelling over Aldersgate', published 'The Whole Booke of Psalmes collected into Englysh metre by T. Starnhold, J. Hopkins and others', and for well over a century this was the sacred song book of the English people. In addition to the new paraphrases included to complete the whole of the psalms, and an enlarged Appendix, some paraphrases used previously were replaced by new translations, and there were a number of new tunes too. Even then, only about one third of the psalms had melodies, the remainder having to borrow. It is interesting to note that it became the custom from this time for theoretical instruction to be given in psalters to help the singers to read music by means of a 'sol-fa' system. In the following year, 1563, John Day produced a harmonised edition with the music in four separate part-books, the Tenor part, as was the custom, having the melody. Known as 'The Whole Psalmes in Foure Partes' it was intended for choirs, and not for the congregations of parish churches who sang the metrical psalms in unison according to Calvinistic practice.

The fact that Sternhold, Hopkins and the other contributors to 'The Whole Booke of Psalmes' made great use of an old ballad metre was undoubtedly a main reason for the popularity of their paraphrases. Many of the old ballads had four-line verses, with alternate lines of four stresses and three, as we see in the following verse from 'The wife of Usher's Well':

> *'They hadna been a week from her,*
> *A week but barely one,*
> *When word came to the carline wife*
> *That her three sons were gone.'*

Compare the metre of the above with that of the first two verses from

Psalm 81 in 'The Whole Booke of Psalmes', an example of the work of John Hopkins:

1. *'Be light and glad, in God rejoice,*
   Which is our strength and stay;
   Be joyful, and lift up your voice
   To Jacob's God I say.

2. *Prepare your instruments most meet*
   Some joyful psalm to sing;
   Strike up with harp and lute so sweet
   On every pleasant string.'

This 'ballad metre' became known in hymnals as Common Metre, generally abbreviated to C.M. and otherwise described as 8.6.8.6. to indicate the number of syllables in each line. So popular has this metre always been with our people and poets that numerous examples readily spring to mind, including that 'skeely' skipper, Sir Patrick Spens, citizen John Gilpin and the Ancient Mariner. We are reminded also of Nahum Tate's hymn, 'While shepherds watched their flocks by night' - one of the few 'human hymns' which the church permitted in the eighteenth century - and the paraphrase by Isaac Watts of Psalm 90 - 'O God, our help in ages past'.

Most of the tunes originally used with the paraphrases of Sternhold and Hopkins were longish ones, many being in double common metre (D.C.M.). Two verses of Psalm 81 (see above) were required for each singing of the tune. Four-line tunes were comparatively unknown in the 1560's, the one we now know as 'St. Michael' (Short metre; S.M. or 6.6.8.6.) being a rare example from that time.

In the 'Oxford Companion to Music' (p. 450), Scholes tells us that during its long life, 'Sternhold and Hopkins' passed with very little change through six hundred editions, 'its phraseology having almost acquired the authority of Holy Writ.' During the remainder of the sixteenth, and almost throughout the seventeenth century, it was the standard book of metrical psalms authorised by the Church of England. Other tune books appeared from time to time with the object of providing alternative settings for the 'Sternhold and Hopkins' paraphrases, settings for example by such distinguished musicians as John Dowland, Giles Farnaby, Thomas Ravenscroft and Orlando Gibbons. Common Metre four-line tunes gradually displaced many of those in Double Common Metre, and it became customary to give each tune a name. Some of these books made a valuable contribution to the development of psalmody, and some introduced new tunes which are still popular today. At different times a few of these publications became companions to 'Sternhold and Hopkins', but none ever achieved the latter's outstanding and continued success. A comprehensive and illustrated account of the history of psalmody and hymnody may be found in the 'Historical Companion to Hymns Ancient and Modern' (Clowes).

With the Commonwealth came the disbanding of choirs and the removal of church organs. The Puritans did not object to music in church, but only to music which was elaborate and to the use of instruments. The singing of metrical psalms was encouraged and we are told that they were often the marching songs of the opposing armies. After the Restoration more settings were published, the most notable being by John Playford of 'English Dancing Master' fame. His remarks on the low standard of church music, mentioned in our last chapter, come from the preface to his 'Psalms and Hymns' of 1671, and his 'Whole Book of Psalms' of 1677 was the first to give all the melodies in the Treble rather than in the Tenor part. The mention of hymns reminds us that, in spite of the attitude of the Church, hymn writing continued. It was towards the end of the seventeenth century that Bishop Ken wrote 'Awake my soul and with the sun', and 'Glory to thee, my God, this night' for the private use of Winchester scholars.

By this time 'Sternhold and Hopkins', the popular favourite for well over a century, was meeting with growing criticism. Many thought that there was little in its pages that was inspired, but much that was mediocre or mere doggerel, a criticism which seems justified when we read the following verses:

'And still like dust before the wind
I drive them under feet;
And sweep them out like filthy dirt
That lieth in the street.'   (Psalm 18. v. 41)

'As men once dead are out of mind,
So am I now forgot;
As little use of me they find
As of a broken pot.'   (Psalm 31. v. 12)

'With shame and great confusion I
Afflicted am full sore;
Yea, so I blush, that all my face
With red is cover'd o'er.'   (Psalm 44. v. 12)

There was a demand for something better and so the Poet Laureate, Nahum Tate, was asked to write new paraphrases, and he had as collaborator Dr. Nicholas Brady, Rector of St. Catherine Cree, London.

Nahum Tate had been responsible for the libretto of Purcell's 'Dido and Aeneas', and at one time was busily engaged in 'improving' Shakespeare's plays. It is said that up to the middle of the last century most people preferred his improved 'King Lear', with a happy ending, to the original. By 1696 Tate and Brady's task was completed, the work was dedicated to King William III and authorised for immediate use. With the publication of this 'New Version of the Psalms of David, Fitted to the Tunes used in Churches', the earlier work of Sternhold and Hopkins became known as the 'Old Version', some of the tunes acquiring the prefix 'old', as for example, the tune set to Psalm 100 which became known as the 'Old Hundredth'.

Although 'Tate and Brady' was a much more scholarly work than 'Sternhold and Hopkins' it was not without its critics. Some stoutly defended the book they had used for years, preferring the known to the unknown. Others spoke up for the new, but Dr. Brady's own congregation refused to use it, and pamphlets objecting to it were published. Church authorities and congregations were alike divided and so the two versions existed side by side as recognised alternatives throughout the eighteenth century, lingering on well into the nineteenth in some places. The second Viscount Halifax (1839-1934) remembered the Hickleton (near Doncaster) church of his boyhood, with its musicians' gallery at the west end. The clerk, a helper in the stables at the Hall, had charge of the music and played the 'cello, whilst a brother played the flute and a nephew the fiddle. In addition to those for Christmas and Easter, Lord Halifax remembered only two hymns being sung - 'Awake my soul' and 'Glory to thee, my God, this night' - but they had the metrical version of the psalms, 'not the later one by Tate and Brady but the earlier version of Sternhold and Hopkins.' (J. G. Lockhart, 'Viscount Halifax' Vol. 1, 1935 Geoffrey Bles).

At first 'Tate and Brady' had no music and confined itself to paraphrases of the psalms in familiar metres so that they could be sung 'to the best and most useful tunes of the Old Version'. In 1700 however, the New Version got its own musical companion when a 'Supplement' was published separately. Including well-known tunes from earlier psalters and music for the Canticles, Creed, Lord's Prayer and Commandments, it also had the words of six hymns, one of which was 'While Shepherds', and some new paraphrases. There had been complaints that the New Version, by keeping to familiar metres, had prevented many of the Old Version tunes in less familiar, or as they were called, 'peculiar' metres (P.M.) from being used. The new paraphrases repaired this omission. Of the other publications appearing about this time the most notable was 'The Divine Companion' (1701) by Henry Playford, the son of John, which was a collection of paraphrases, hymns and anthems, including music by John Blow, William Croft and Jeremiah Clarke.

The outstanding feature, however, of eighteenth century Christian expression in this country was that of hymn writing, a feature inspired by the Independent minister Isaac Watts, the creator of the modern hymn, and later by the Church of England clergymen, John and Charles Wesley, who saw the hymn as a powerful aid to their evangelism, and still later in the century by the combined work of the poet William Cowper and the ex-slave trader, John Newton. Their inspiration led numerous 'lesser lights' to take up the pen, and multitudes of their fellow countrymen to lift up their voices. At first their hymns were sung to existing psalm tunes, but it was not long before the different dissenting bodies desired to have, not only their own hymnals, but their own books of tunes as well. The first Methodist tune book was 'A Collection of Tunes Set to music as they are commonly sung at the Foundery' (1742), so called because John Wesley's first London meeting house was on the site of a disused iron foundry. Many other tune books followed, books with new tunes, old tunes, good tunes and bad tunes, with tunes adapted from popular songs and oratorios, with florid tunes so beloved by chapel choirs, and even with tunes written by Handel at the request of Charles Wesley.

Though hymn and tune books grew in number and hymn-singing in popularity the attitude of the Church of England was more or less unchanged. The intrusion of hymns, apart from one or two for special occasions, was resented by the Establishment and there was a strong determination to prevent psalmody from being overwhelmed by hymnody. As late as 1819 the congregation of St. Paul's Church, Sheffield, objected to a new collection of psalms and hymns introduced by the vicar, and an appeal against the book was made to the Diocesan Court. Only the diplomatic intervention of the Archbishop prevented a serious crisis, for he offered to sanction another selection if the offending book was withdrawn. As long as such an attitude prevailed it was only by making psalmody more appealing that the attraction of non-conformist hymnody could be counteracted, and towards the end of the eighteenth century several books, including Edward Miller's 'The Psalms of David', were published with this object in mind. There were private attempts at reform too. The Rev. William Mason, Precentor of York, whom we met in Chapter Four, made a partial revision of 'Sternhold and Hopkins' and had it printed privately in 1783 for the use of his congregation at Aston. Copies may be seen in the Minster Library, York.

Proposals for printing Miller's 'Psalms of David' by subscription appeared in the 'York Courant' of Tuesday March 20th 1790. A list of subscribers' names was to be printed with the book, the price was seven shillings and sixpence to subscribers (37½p), ten and sixpence to non-subscribers (52½p), and delivery was promised for July. A similar notice on July 20th added that the list of subscribers already included the names of their Royal Highnesses, The Prince of Wales and the Duke of York, together with many of the Nobility and Gentry, and also a respectable number of Bishops, Deans and Archdeacons. Delivery of the book, however, was postponed to September. By August 10th the 'Courant' told of a subscription list 'now upwards of 900' and a month later, on September 7th it reported that the figure had passed one thousand, that the book was 'Recommended by His Majesty' and the subscription list would close at the end of September.

On November 13th Dr. Miller respectfully informed the subscribers by means of an advertisement in the 'Yorkshire Journal' that the book would be ready on December 1st, but non-subscribers must wait a little longer, because the engraved plates were worn out by numerous impressions for the 3,500 subscription copies, and a second set of plates was being prepared. The non-subscribers, however, did not have long to wait, for the 'York Courant' of January 25th 1791 announced publication that day of 'The Psalms of David' at ten shillings and sixpence, and also publication of 'Words Only' editions, price sixpence on common paper, one shilling and sixpence on fine wove paper, and a few octavo copies on superfine wove paper at three shillings and sixpence. The work was dedicated to 'The Most Reverend Father in God, William, Archbishop of York' and, as already stated, printed and published by Edward's nephew, William R. B. Miller at No. 5, Old Bond Street. A month later, on February 22nd 1791 the 'Courant' advertised the publication of the second edition, 'the first, consisting of 4,500 copies, being already sold', and also a second edition of the words. By September 27th 1805 the 8th Music addition was being advertised in the 'Doncaster Gazette', and it appears that a new edition of the 'Words Only' was required almost yearly, for in 1814, a 22nd edition was published. Sales slowed appreciably after that date, the 24th edition of the words was being sold in 1825, 'printed by assignment from William Miller for Geo. B. Whittaker, Ave Maria Lane', and in 1842, Whittaker & Co., of the same address, were selling the 26th edition.

On the lower half of the engraved title page of the Music edition is a vignette showing King David on a flowered mound, his right hand supporting an Irish harp, while his left hand holds a scroll inscribed 'Psalms of David'. Leaning against the harp is a small oval medallion with a portrait. The border of the medallion is inscribed 'EDWARDUS MILLER', and scattered on the mound are two open music books and a sheet of music paper. The next page carries the dedication and then there are twelve pages of Preface in which the writer discusses the unsatisfactory state of congregational singing and suggests means of improvement. He

PSALMS OF DAVID
for the Use of
PARISH CHURCHES

The WORDS Selected from the Verfion of TATE & BRADY

BY

The Rev. George Hay Drummond

THE MUSIC

Selected Adapted & Composed

By Edward Miller Mus Doct

"Sing ye Praifes with underftanding"

LONDON.

Printed & Sold by Preston at his Wholesale Warehouses, 97. Strand.

Price 12. 0

Title-page, 'The Psalms of David'
(An early 19th-century edition).

condemns the slow syllabic drawling of the metrical psalms, the practice of 'lining out', and the custom of leaving the choice of words and music to the clerk, even when there is an organist. He then points out that in 'Psalms of David' the choice is no longer left to the clerk, and that it is the first publication of congregational psalmody to appear since the Reformation with a regular arrangement of Words and Music adapted for every Sunday throughout the year. He then describes the methods adopted in his own parish for improving the singing, including the half-hour practices before morning and evening services, and also on Wednesday evenings. Following the Preface is a page of 'Foreign Words', another advertising the author's works, and then thirty-three pages of names of persons, parishes, choirs and societies responsible for subscribing to the 3,420 copies. Both the 'York Courant' and the 'Yorkshire Journal' later reported (February, 1791) that the list of subscribers to Dr. Miller's 'Psalms' was supposed to contain more names than had ever before appeared in any book published in this kingdom, but the 'Doncaster Gazette', writing of Miller's death in the issue of September 18th 1807, said that his list of subscribers was inferior only to that of Pope's 'Homer'. An Index comes next and then the 116 pages of Words and Music.

In his 'History of Doncaster' (p. 88) Edward tells how his collaboration with the vicar, in writing 'The Psalms of David', came about. In 1785, at the age of 24, the Rev. George Hay Drummond, third son of the Hon. Robert Hay Drummond (Archbishop of York, 1761-1777), and grandson of the Earl of Kinnoul who owned the Brodsworth estates, became Vicar of Doncaster. He held the position until 1790, when he exchanged the living for that of nearby Brodsworth. Sometime during his five years at Doncaster, 'observing one sabbath day, that his clerk had chosen both the words and tune of a psalm so improperly as to occasion laughter in some part of the congregation; told me, that in order to remedy such an abuse in future, he would immediately employ himself in selecting the best stanzas in each psalm, from the version of Tate and Brady, and arrange them for every Sunday and festival throughout the year, provided I would adapt them to proper music. I was instantly struck with the idea, and in performing my part, generally made choice of the most popular of our old and venerable melodies long used in the established church of England.' Although this quotation mentions the vicar using the best stanzas from *each* psalm he did not do so. The whole one hundred and fifty psalms as paraphrased in 'Sternhold and Hopkins' or 'Tate and Brady' must have appeared out-facing to the large numbers who found difficulty in reading, and so he made their task much easier by using not more than half the psalms and then only selecting three or four verses from each. This meant that in allotting two paraphrases to each Sunday morning of the year, one to each evening, and some to

Festivals and Fasts, there was considerable repetition. The first four verses of Psalm 106, for example, appear on five different Sundays, the first verses of Psalm 8 on four Sundays, and there are more than a dozen examples of the same words being used at least three times. Probably the vicar, realising the great number of poor readers in the country, deliberately limited the number of his selections in the hope that frequent repetition would ensure familiarity, aid memorisation, and thus lead to improved reading and increased participation. Generally, but not in every instance, when a selection of words is repeated, the same tune is used.

Edward Miller adopted a similar attitude. In his 'History of Doncaster' (p. 89) he tells us that no difficult music should be used in parochial psalmody, the tunes should be simple and easy, and during the singing the congregation should be standing. He chose only 37 tunes and as two of these, ('Leeds' and 'Proper 149th') were variants of two others included ('St. Anne' and 'Hanover'), there were actually only 35 different tunes, to which must be added the music for a Funeral Hymn which did not have a name. More than half were in Common Metre, more than a quarter in Long Metre, and the remainder either in Short or Peculiar Metre. His selection had a sound basis of the well-established and widely-known, from tunes going back to the Genevan Psalter of 1551, Est's 'Psalms' of 1592, Ravenscroft's 'Psalmes' of 1621, to those by Carey, Croft and Jeremiah Clarke. There were ten new tunes in the thirty-five, seven by Miller himself, two by Dr. Burney and one by Charles Dibdin, and there were also a few 'arrangements', notably fragments from 'Messiah' and 'Saul' condensed into Common Metre. Writing in the Preface about the new tunes Miller said that he hoped they would be found 'neither so dry, nor uninteresting as some of those in mere counter-point of the ancients, nor so ballad-like and indecorous as many which are now sung in the tabernacles of modern Methodists'. It is remarkable that nineteen of his thirty-five selected tunes were still to be found in 'Hymns, Ancient and Modern' well into this century, and eighteen of them are in the present Revised Edition of that work. Only two of the new tunes, Miller's 'Rockingham' and 'Galway' are now sung regularly, though for a time his 'Hatfield' was also popular. In 'Psalms of David' he describes 'Rockingham' as 'part of a melody taken from a hymn tune'. The hymn tune was 'Tunbridge', (10.11.10.11) which appeared in a book called 'Psalmody in Miniature' in 1778, and it is said that underneath this tune, in his copy of that book, Miller wrote, 'Would make a good long metre'. He reconstructed 'Tunbridge', with its four lines of alternate ten and eleven syllables into 'Rockingham', with lines all of eight syllables, but it was not until 1854 that this popular tune became associated with the words 'When I survey the wond'rous cross'. As already mentioned 'Gallway' or 'Galway' was dedicated to Lord

Evening
Pſalm 62. Verses 6. 7. 8. 11.
Rockingham. L. M.

7
God does his ſaving health diſpenſe,
And flowing bleſsings daily ſend;
He is my fortreſs and defence;
On him my ſoul ſhall ſull depend.

8
In him, ye people, always truſt,
Before his throne pour out your hearts;
For God the merciful and juſt,
His timely aid to us imparts.

11
The Lord has oft his will expreſs'd
And I this truth have fully known,
To be of boundleſs pow'r poſſeſs'd
Belongs of right to God alone.

Psalm Tune - 'Rockingham', from Miller's 'Psalms of David'.

Tunbridge. P.M.

Psalm Tune - 'Tunbridge'. (By permission of 'Hymns Ancient and Modern').

85

Galway of Serlby Hall, and 'Hatfield' may have received its name from a nearby village, or from the previous Vicar of Doncaster, the Rev. George Hatfeild, who often wrote his name with the 'e' before the 'i' although his family belonged to Hatfield village. The dedication of Miller's 'Doncaster' needs no explanation, and it is interesting to note that with this tune he gives an interlude to be played between the verses, a custom he favoured and which was in common use. He did object, however, to 'extraneous flourishes or in running up and down the keys at the end of every line'. All the music is in short score with the melody in the Treble - Miller believed that the congregational singing should be in unison - and the Bass is 'correctly figured for the organ'. Between Treble and Bass are small notes which complete the chords. These are not for singing but to help accompanists who cannot realise a figured bass. Miller was thinking of ladies at their harpsichords, for he hoped his book would also be regarded as a 'Sunday Evening Companion'. To complete the work there is an Appendix of twenty-four pages in which most of the tunes appear again, but this time chiefly in three parts and at a lower pitch, 'for the practice of country choirs'. Between the melody-line and the bass part is one for the Counter-tenor or Tenor, but no accompaniment. The subscription copy ends on page 142, but the sixth and subsequent editions had an Addenda of five new melodies, one of which, 'Bangor' is in the present 'Ancient and Modern, Revised Edition'. ('Doncaster Gazette', December 8th 1797).

In the years immediately following the publication of 'The Psalms of David' there were many references to it in the press, a few of which, all taken from the 'Doncaster Journal', are given here. (The 'Doncaster Journal', published weekly, succeeded the 'Yorkshire Journal' on February 12th 1791). The issue of February 26th 1791 told of a Chester book-seller who received the following note from a clerk in the country -

'Sur, you wun plase to sond me the klark of our parrish the salms of Davy, new aversion, with a pitched pipe'.

On the 9th of July of the same year the paper reported: 'It is with pleasure we hear, that the Rev. Mr. Drummond's and Dr. Miller's elegant selection of Psalms, which was first introduced in our church, has already been adopted by upwards of a hundred parish churches in the Kingdom'.

On January 21st 1792 the 'Journal' stated that 'His Majesty has been graciously pleased to order £25 to be sent to Dr. Miller of this town, in token of approbation of his late publication of the "Psalms of David"'. By this time Barrel or Psalmodic Organs were to be found in many of the smaller churches. Generally an organ of this type had two or three interchangeable barrels with about ten psalm tunes on each. When new tunes were published as, for example, 'Rockingham' and 'Galway' and others in 'Psalms of David', it was necessary to buy an additional barrel or barrels equipped with these tunes. On December 3rd 1791 the paper advertised 'Psalmodic Organs for the use of small Churches or Chapels, where Large Organs and Organists cannot be supported, and to which are adapted Dr. Miller's late publication of Psalm Tunes, with corresponding short interludes, for every Sunday throughout the year'. The cost of organ and barrels was from 24 to 48 guineas. (£25.20 to £50.40).

In Words and Music editions for non-subscribers there was not, of course, the list of subscribers' names and neither was there a Preface. What could be regarded as an enlarged version of the Preface was published separately by Wm. Miller in 1791 with the title of 'Thoughts on the Present Performance of Psalmody in the Established Church of England, addressed to the Clergy'. Later, Dr. Miller published a four-part version of the tunes called 'Psalms of David for Choirs of Singers'. There is a copy of this in the British Library which belonged to the church of St. Peter Mancroft, Norwich. Written on it are the words: 'Presented . . . . . . by Dr. Miller of Doncaster, a native of this parish. Thos. Eaton, Churchwarden, 1805', and lower down, 'By the Author, born in this Parish, October 30th, 1735'.

THE REV. GEORGE HAY DRUMMOND
Vicar of Doncaster, 1785-90.

Chapter Eleven

The 'Doncaster Journal and Yorkshire Advertiser' printed the following quotation in the issue of February 19th 1791 -

'Extract of a letter from Mr. Miller to his father, Dr. Miller of this town, dated at Calcutta, August 4th 1790. Received by the "Houghton".

We are at war here and money not to be had - Our army, with General Meadows at the head, and in the highest order, is now in Tippoo's country. - An engagement has not yet happened, though daily expected. - It is supposed we shall take the whole country, and restore it to the antient kings of Mysore. - Tippoo has shewn not the least of his former activity; but, indeed, there are at present such various reports that there is no knowing how to judge of affairs. If we be fortunate, our acquisitions will be great, as the English will then be the most powerful government in Hindostan; nor is there much doubt of our success, as we never had before in India such an army for force or equipment. - Nothing but the most rigid economy reigns here. - In the last five months there has not been a concert, ball, general supper, or one public amusement. - However this is not a place in which Roman severity, or the sternness of republican abstemiousness can be relished. - Sir William Jones is much pleased with your Morceau delicat. - Mr. Hewett has received me most cordially. - I shall pay my respects to him at Constai. - And then my dear father, I hope prosperous winds will soon waft me to England, and that I shall for ever bid adieu to this dull, spiritless and enervating country.'

William Edward Miller, born in Doncaster on June 1st 1766, baptized on July 10th, was seven years old when his mother died. He must have received a musical education from his father, for by the time he was fourteen he was performing in public in Doncaster, as this notice from the 'York Courant' of April 17th 1781 shows -

'At the ANNUAL FESTIVAL of the MUSICAL SOCIETY
at the MANSION HOUSE on Thursday, May 3rd, 1781,
A GRAND CONCERT
To be conducted by Mr. Miller
The 1st Violin with a Solo Concerto by Mr. Miller Jnr.
Between the instrumental pieces a number of
Chorusses, Glees, Catches, etc., will be performed by the
Gentlemen of the Society, assisted by those of
others in the neighbourhood.
The whole to conclude with the
Grand Coronation Anthem of Mr. Handell,
God Save the King.
After the Concert a Ball.
Concert begins at 7 p.m. Tickets, 2/6 at the Angel,
the Red Lion, or Mr. Miller's house.'

We learn more of William Edward's early life from the Rev. T. Alexander Seed's book - 'Norfolk Street Wesleyan Chapel, Sheffield' (Jarrold, 1907) - according to whose account he went to London when he was sixteen and lived there for about two years. His gay and extravagant mode of living, however, caused his father to stop his allowance, whereupon he sailed for India, which became his home until he was twenty-five. During that time a song he had written - 'When present in our charmer's sight' - appeared in his father's 'Elements of Thorough Bass and Composition' (1787), and his name - 'W. E. Miller of Calcutta' - was printed in the list of subscribers to 'Psalms of David' in 1790. Sir William Jones mentioned in the letter was an Oriental scholar and translator of Persian poetry, and from 1783 to 1794, Judge of the High Court at Calcutta. One of his poems translated from the Persian was printed in the 'Doncaster Journal' of August 2nd 1794. The 'morceau delicat' remains a mystery.

William Nathan Wrighte Hewett is known to have been in India in 1786, but by 1794 was living at Bilham House, six miles from Doncaster. Later he lived in the town itself at 18, South Parade, and in 1808 was a Lieutenant-Colonel in the Militia, commanding the Wath Wood Infantry. His grandson, Vice-Admiral Sir William Nathan Wrighte Hewett was, in 1857, one of the first recipients of the Victoria Cross.

When William Edward arrived in India in 1784 the British had been fighting for supremacy for more than forty years. Clive had had his victories, returned home and died, and Warren Hastings, the Governor

General, was soon to be succeeded by Lord Cornwallis. Tippoo Sahib had become Sultan of Mysore on the death of his father in 1782 whilst the first Mysore War was being fought. This ended with a treaty in 1784, but five years later Tippoo attacked the Rajah of Travancore, an ally of the British, and the second Mysore War began. In 1791 Tippoo was besieged in his capital, Seringapatam, and forced to cede half his dominion. Hostilities broke out again in 1799 and Tippoo, after suffering two defeats, again retreated to the capital where he perished when it was attacked and taken.

The Rev. Mr. Seed adds that when 'W.E.' was first in India he made much money as a professional musician, but lost it later and returned home with little but a Cremona violin that had been given to him by Tippoo Sahib and which was said to be worth three hundred guineas. Hatfield, in his 'Historical Notices of Doncaster', (Vol. 1, p. 382) sounds a litte doubtful about this happening -

'The tradition in current vogue used to be that young Miller, having heard that in the court of Tippoo Sahib an exquisite instrument was in use by one of the Sultan's band, and having pushed his way to Seringapatam, he so enchanted the Sovereign by his performance as to obtain possession of the prize.'

It seems strange for such a gift to have been made during the time that Tippoo was either at war with Britain or having to submit to British demands. Perhaps the instrument, if it ever existed, was not so much a gift as one of the spoils of war.

True to his word, William Edward soon sailed for home, arriving some time towards the end of 1791. He gave the first concert on his return to members of the Anacreontic Society in London. This was a gathering of aristocratic musical amateurs who met to sing Glees and Catches, have supper and listen to professional performers. Their song, 'Anacreon in Heaven', with music by John Stafford Smith, was always sung at their gatherings, and sung likewise at the meetings of Anacreontic Societies in America. An American, Francis Scott Key, used this tune for a poem he had written, and thus 'The Star Spangled Banner' was born, now the official anthem of the United States. On January 7th 1792 the 'Doncaster Journal' reported -

'The London papers spoke in highest terms of Mr. Miller's first public performance in England at the Anacreontic Society. As it must be gratifying to the friends of Dr. Miller, we have copied the following account of his son from "The Times" -

'His Concerto on the violin bespoke all the skill and execution of a master, blended with all the modest diffidence of the scholar. The adagio movement evinced taste and science; his tones had great power and sweetness, and his shake would not have disgraced either a Janorick or Cramer......Cramer, who in a preceding Quartetto had "lapped the souls of his hearers in Elysium", was, much to the credit of his liberality, among the warmest of his applauders.'

Later in 1792 William Edward settled in Norfolk Street, Sheffield, as a professional musician. From Tuesday June 5th to Friday June 8th of that year, he was the Leader of the Band and Solo Violinist at a four-day Festival conducted by his father in Louth. The mornings were occupied by the performances of 'Judas Maccabeus', 'Messiah', 'Jehovah' and 'Messiah' again. This was the first performance of 'Jehovah', described as an Oratorio consisting of the favourite works of Handel, selected by Dr. Miller. On both Tuesday and Thursday evenings there was a Ball in the Town Hall, on Wednesday evening a performance of 'Acis and Galatea', and the proceedings concluded on the Friday evening with a Grand Miscellaneous Concert. The 'Doncaster Journal' of June 16th reported that Mr. Miller's Solo Concerto at the final concert evinced the truth of the character given him in London.

It was about a month after this Festival that Lois Miller died (July 7th 1792), leaving William Edward the sole survivor of the seven daughters and three sons of Edward and Elizabeth. In the same year, on December 13th, he married Mary, the daughter of Alderman John Dunhill, innkeeper of Doncaster, who was Mayor in 1790 and 1797.

Father and son appeared together again in the two following years, for 'W.E.' played a Solo Concerto on the Violin and a Sonata on the Grand Pianoforte at the Mansion House on the Friday morning of Race Week (September 27th 1793), and on Friday, July 11th 1794, there was an important one-day Festival of Music, under the direction of Dr. Miller, at the opening of the new organ in St. James' Chapel (later Church), Sheffield. This was not only a new organ, but the first to be erected in that chapel, and William Edward became the first organist.

The morning concert followed a familiar pattern, with Edward directing sacred items from the oratorios of Handel, and William Edward leading the band and playing a Concerto on the organ. An additional feature was the singing of Psalm 100 with instrumental accompaniment. This, according to the 'Yorkshire, Nottinghamshire and Lincolnshire Gazette' of July 19th, 'had a sublime effect, and most of the company, with due reverence, devoutly joined in it standing.' The evening's entertainment in the theatre, however, was quite unusual. After praising Mr. Miller's most admirable playing on the Violin and Grand Pianoforte, the paper told of the Grand Procession in honour of

Lord Howe's glorious victory on the first of June, particularly mentioning the martial appearance of the Light Horse, the banners and flags of the different societies in Sheffield, and the Loyal Independent Sheffield Volunteers and their Band, all in new uniforms. The report added that a choir of men and women singing 'See the conquering hero comes' produced a fine effect, much heightened by a grand transparency with the inscription, 'Britannia and her conquering hero, HOWE', under which -'Mr. Meredith, with true pathos, sang, "When Britons first at Heav'n's command", accompanied by all the House'. Also in the programme were two patriotic songs written especially for the Festival, the first having music by Dr. Miller. Given below is the fourth and last verse of this song, the words by His Grace, the Duke of Leeds:

> *'Hail happy Britain, favour'd isle!*
> *Where Freedom, Arts and Commerce smile!*
> *Long may thy GEORGE in glory prove*
> *The transports of a nation's love!*
> *Long reign to guard the blest decree,*
> *That "Britons ever shall be free."'*

The above song was later published with an accompaniment for a Military Band.

The second song, with music by W. E. Miller and words by the Earl of Mulgrave, had three verses, with the following chorus:

> *'Now, danger past, we'll drink and joke -*
> *Sing, "Rule Britannia", "Hearts of Oak"!*
> *And toast before each martial tune -*
> *"Howe, and the glorious first of June!"'*

The French Revolution at first aroused some sympathy in this country, but the proclamation of a republic, the massacres, and the beheading of the King transformed much of the sympathy into hostility. Early in 1793 England joined the First Coalition against France, along with Prussia, Austria, Spain and Holland. To the surprise of many the French fought with considerable success, and Howe's glorious victory was the first bright spot in the campaign. Throughout these French Revolutionary Wars and the later Napoleonic Wars the conquest of India continued.

William Edward, though appointed organist at St. James' Chapel, was soon attracted by the singing at Norfolk Street Wesleyan Chapel and before long was a member of the Wesleyan Society and a local preacher. In 1799 he became a Wesleyan Minister. On taking this step we are told by the Rev. Mr. Seed that he laid aside his violin, which had, he thought, become to him a snare. For the next quarter of a century he laboured in many Wesleyan circuits, including Whitby, Sheffield, Rochdale, Manchester, Leeds and Cromford.

In this chapter pride of place has been given to William Edward's story, including his homecoming and the subsequent collaboration of father and son. Now we turn to Edward again and tell of his own activities during the last decade of the eighteenth century. It was mentioned in the last chapter that Subscription Copies of 'Psalms of David' contained a one-page advertisement of the author's publications. One item told of the forthcoming appearance in May 1791 of Opera Seven, 'Twenty-four Exercises in all the Major and Minor Keys, for the improvement of Performers on the Piano Forte or Harpsichord'. Mystery surrounds this work, which was intended as an Appendix to 'Institutes of Music', for no copy of it can be traced, and it may be that it was never published.

On the other hand, Opera Eight, which was also mentioned in the advertisement, appeared later that year, with 'Opera VIII' clearly printed on the Title-page. It was, 'Twelve Progressive Lessons for the Piano Forte or Harpsichord, with an Accompaniment for the Violin or Flute', described in the 'Doncaster Journal' of December 3rd 1791 as a sequel to the 'Institutes of Music', and published, priced ten shillings and sixpence, (52½p) by William Miller, 5, Old Bond Street, Bookseller to the Duke of Clarence. The pieces, all of two or three short movements, provided slightly more difficult material for students who had mastered the practical section of the 'Institutes', and gave them the opportunity of combining with other instruments. Opera Nine, Edward's next major work, did not appear for another six years, but in the meantime he composed a number of songs, several of which, apart from their musical interest, throw light on conditions at home and abroad towards the turn of the century.

In the years immediately before and after 1790 history was being made in a small factory in Fishergate, quite near to the Parish Church and Dr. Miller's residence. Its owner, a most remarkable man, was Edmund Cartwright, priest, poet, farmer and inventor. He was born at Marnham in Nottinghamshire in 1743, and in 1772 married Alice Whitaker of Doncaster, the daughter of a former Mayor of the town. In 1785 Cartwright invented and patented the first power-loom. Meeting with little enthusiasm and some hostility he decided to build his own spinning and weaving factory on land in Fishergate. Thus Doncaster was the home of the first commercial power-looms, and after development and improvement, Cartwright's invention became universally used.

In 1789 he invented a wool-combing machine which in its crudest form could do the work of twenty men, and on which subsequent machines were modelled. Because of its lashing movements the workers named it Big Ben after a well-known prize-fighter. Cartwright was a man before his time, and after spending £30,000 on his inventions, became bankrupt in 1793, living long enough however, to see his ideas making other people wealthy. Cartwright Hall in Bradford was named in his honour and until recently there were Cartwright and Whitaker Streets in Doncaster. In 1806 the University of Oxford conferred the Degree of Doctor of Divinity on the inventor, and in 1809 Parliament voted him the sum of £10,000. He died in 1823. It is said that after the successful invention of his wool-combing machine he encouraged his Doncaster workpeople to have a procession in honour of Bishop Blaize. This Armenian bishop was regarded as the patron saint of wool-combers for he was cruelly martyred about 316 A.D., being scratched to death by wool-dressers' combs. His statue stands outside the Wool Exchange in Bradford, and it was customary before the Industrial Revolution for processions in his honour to be held from time to time in centres of the woollen industry, including Leeds, Bradford and Halifax. A picture of such a procession appears in George Walker's 'Costume of Yorkshire', (1814). The wool-masters on horseback, their sons, apprentices and workpeople, together with those arrayed as the King, Queen, members of the Royal Family, Bishop Blaize, Jason, Shepherds and Shepherdesses, paraded through the streets to some place where the day could be given over to jollification. A long poem was recited which began -

> *'Hail to the day whose kind auspicious rays*
> *Deigned first to smile on famous Bishop Blaize.'*

No doubt the Doncaster celebration of 1792 was on a smaller scale, although we are told that an ox was roasted, large quantities of plum pudding consumed, and there was a plentiful flow of a drink known as 'brown nappy'. The Doncaster poem was certainly quite different, for it was written by Matthew Charlton, one of Cartwright's workpeople. Here is the first of its four verses -

> *'Come all ye master-combers, and hear of new Big Ben,*
> *He'll comb more wool in one day than fifty of your men,*
> *With their hand-combs and comb-pots and such old-fashion'd*
> > *ways;*
> *There'll be no more occasion for old Bishop Blaize.'*

The music for this was by Edward Miller, and Hatfield ('Historical Notices', Vol. 2, p. 317) says that for several years it was a favourite and popular air among the lower classes in the town and neighbourhood.

The verses of an unknown writer, which Edward set to music in the year following, were in a different mood, a mood not of merriment but of mourning. On October 26th 1793 the 'Doncaster Journal' reported the trial and execution of the Queen of France, and in the following issue printed a poem called, 'The Queen of France. Her lamentation before her execution.' After a short recitative the first verse began –

> *'O murder'd King! from yon bright sky*
> *Look down, and see my wretched state!*
> *No friend to help - no husband nigh,*
> *Expos'd to savage Tygers hate......'*

The paper added that this song had already been sung at 'The Handelian Concert', and the music was by Dr. Miller. Unfortunately the date and place of this event are not mentioned.

In 1794, as we saw earlier in this chapter, the mood of the country was martial, with a great outburst of patriotic fervour after the Glorious First of June. The King and Country needed men for the forces, men for the defence of the homeland, and money to meet the cost. An advertisement in the 'Yorkshire, Nottinghamshire and Lincolnshire Gazette' on November 1st said that two French Horn men, two for the Clarinet, two Fifers and two Drummers, all good performers, were required immediately to engage for three months on the recruiting business. The issue of December 20th told of a man being set in the stocks at Doncaster on the previous Sunday, for being intoxicated during the time of Divine Service. He was the schoolmaster and parish clerk of a neighbouring village who had enlisted for a soldier the previous evening. Volunteer Corps of Infantry and Cavalry were also being formed for internal defence and security, and subscription lists opened in order to provide the necessary equipment. The 'Gazette' of May 31st 1794 reported a meeting the previous Saturday in Doncaster for the purpose of boosting the morale of everyone, obtaining subscriptions from as many as possible, and encouraging members of the gentry and other 'substantial inhabitants' to volunteer to defend their country. This gathering was addressed by Dr. Miller who told his audience that the war was one of Christianity against Atheism, a war on which our very existence depended, and a war of men against monsters whose streets were crimsoned with the blood of their guiltless countrymen. He asked his listeners to give whatever assistance they could to counteract the dark desires of wicked men. He also set another patriotic poem to music. Called 'War and Justice' it was for the Yorkshire Cavalry and the Sheffield Volunteers, and the words appeared in the 'Gazette' of December 20th. Its unknown author was in the thick of the fighting before the end of the first verse –

'Fierce, still fiercer raged the battle,
Trumpets sounding,
Bullets bounding,
Dismal groans,
Piercing moans,
Lightning flashing,
Faulchions clashing,
Sheets of fire and clouds of smoke
The darkened atmosphere does choke.'

It was in this year also that Edward became a Freeman of Doncaster.

Judging from newspaper reports his musical activities in the years immediately following 1794 were fewer in number and certainly less warlike. A Festival he conducted in St. Paul's Church, Sheffield, on Wednesday, September 21st 1796 was entirely devoted to Handel, with 'Judas Maccabeus' in the morning and 'Messiah' in the evening. It was about this time too that he wrote the words and music of a 'Song for Free Masons'. This was performed on April 24th 1797 in the Free Masons' Hall, London, at the Anniversary Feast of the Free Masons' Charity for Female Children, and the 'Gazette' of April 28th printed the words in full. Of the songs mentioned in this chapter, with music by Edward Miller, only that with words by the Duke of Leeds appears to have been published. Later in 1797, on December 8th, the 'Doncaster Gazette' announced the publication by Longman and Broderip of Opera Nine, which was briefly mentioned earlier in this chapter. This was 'Sixteen Easy Voluntaries for the Organ, Nine of them being of a proper length to perform at Church before the first lesson, also a Voluntary for Christmas Day, one for Easter Day and one for Funerals.' The price was seven shillings and sixpence (37½p). In the Introduction, Edward expresses the hope that these little pieces, mostly in two sections and composed for one of his pupils, will prove useful to young organists and others. He adds - 'As the original Intention of the first Voluntary, in our Parish Churches was, merely to give the Clergyman Time to find the Lessons; this Performance ought never to exceed four, or at the farthest, five Minutes. The length of Time too often employed in the aforesaid Voluntary, has been generally a matter of Complaint.' He again attacks 'the long, and frequently extraneous Interludes' between the verses of the metrical psalms and urges young organists 'to repeat, only the last line of each Stanza by way of Interlude, till they acquire more knowledge in scientific Modulation.' Four of the voluntaries marked 'Full Organ' afford organists ample scope, 'for the display of their Finger and musical Abilities . . . . on the dismission of the Congregation'.

Returning briefly to the year 1796, and visiting the Nottingamshire town of Tuxford, about twenty-five miles from Doncaster, we find an interesting item in the parish registers -

'Edward Miller, Doctor of Music, of the Parish of Doncaster in the county of York, widower, and Margaret Lloyd Edwards of the Parish of Tuxford, spinster, were married in this church by Licence this twenty-ninth Day of December in the year One Thousand Seven Hundred and Ninety Six by me John Wootton, Officiat Minister.

This marriage was solemnized by us   Edward Miller
                                      Margaret Lloyd Edwards
             In the presence of   George Daft
                                      Johannes Woottonius'.

It would appear that one witness did not get to the church in time and the minister, suitably translated, took his place. The 'Gazette' reported that Miss Edwards was the daughter of the late Rev. D. Edwards of Ipswich, and this suggests that perhaps the two families knew each other in East Anglia. Very little is known of the bride and Edward never mentions her in his writings except in his Will. She outlived him by more than thirty years and died near London on May 8th 1838.

*   *   *   *   *

A dip into the pages of two small books brings this chapter to a close. The first, no more than a notebook and never published, may be seen in the Department of Manuscripts at the British Library. It was the work of John Wall Callcott (1766-1821), organist and composer of glees and catches, and the faded brown ink tells about the 'Musical Graduates', a society of professors of music which was established in London on November 24th 1790. At that time the writing and singing of glees and catches was very popular. The Glee Club, founded in 1787, was an immediate success and this led a few of its members to suggest that there were sufficient musical graduates, in and around the capital, to constitute a select party which could meet throughout the year at each member's house in turn. This idea was welcomed by the small number eligible for membership, about ten in all, and the first meeting was held at number 480, opposite Craven Street, Strand, the home of Dr. Samuel Arnold, organist and composer to His Majesty's Chapel Royal, who in 1793 became organist at Westminster Abbey. The fourth meeting was at Dr. Burney's in Chelsea College, and in 1791 Haydn became a member of this select group after receiving the degree of Doctor of Music at the University of Oxford. He attended the eighth meeting on October 26th 1791 at the Grosvenor Gate home of Dr. Dupuis, organist and composer to His Majesty. On June 20th 1792, prior to his leaving England, Haydn entertained the graduates to dinner at Parsloe's in St. James Street, and on this occasion Salomon, the famous violinist and impresario, was admitted as a friend and interpreter - 'Dr. Haydn having not made sufficient progress with the English tongue.' Among the other members were Benjamin Cooke, who was organist at Westminster Abbey before Arnold, and Sir William Parsons, a minor musician of whom it was said that he was knighted, 'more on the score of his merits than on the merits of his scores.' Originally each meeting began with a dinner which was followed by a number of toasts - The King and Constitution; The Queen and Royal Family; 'Viva la Musica'; The Two Universities; Absent Brethren - and then there was a discussion on some musical topic. After a time, however, the discussion was omitted, for as Callcott wrote, 'there were moments when the power of wine conquered that of reason.' Occasionally country graduates were invited and Callcott records the attendance, as a guest, of Dr. Miller.

The second book, 'A History of Retford', a small hard-backed volume of 246 pages, was written by John S. Piercy, a Retford schoolmaster, and printed in that town by F. Hodson in 1828. In his chapter on the parish church of St. Swithin, East Retford, Piercy tells of its first organ, which came from the theatre at Newark. It was erected in the church in 1770 and replaced by a new instrument in 1797. He also gives a list of the organists of that church, from which the following is an extract -

'July 28th, 1781   Mr. I. Goodlad
July 18th, 1791   Dr. Miller
October 8th, 1797   Mr. John Gildon.'

It is most unlikely that there were two Dr. Millers, both organists, living within twenty miles of each other, and there is no reason to doubt the accuracy of Piercy's statement, for he was writing only twenty years after Edward's death and had access to church records which, unfortunately, have since disappeared.

Most probably Edward had one, or perhaps more than one pupil living within easy reach of Retford, who could play for the Sunday services, he himself only riding over for special occasions, when one of his Doncaster pupils would take his place at St. George's. No doubt he received the salaries from both churches and his pupils' tuition fees also. It must be realised that in the eighteen miles between Retford and Doncaster, and in the surrounding countryside also, there would be no other church which possessed a keyboard organ.

Chapter Twelve

The new century dawned, with Edward in his 65th year, still actively employed as organist, teacher and writer, and soon also to achieve success as local historian. He seems, however, to have virtually ceased his work at concerts and festivals, for the papers only report his participation in two such events during the last decade of his life. The first, described by the 'Doncaster Gazette' of April 19th 1799 as a Military Concert, was held under his direction in the Mansion House on the 24th of that month.

The martial nature of some of the items is understood when we remember that sixteen years were still to elapse before the Napoleonic Wars ended, fighting continued in India, and there had been rebellion in Ireland. Fortunately the morale of the country had been strengthened, even if only temporarily, by recent naval victories at Cape St. Vincent, Camperdown and the Nile.

Part One of the programme included Arne's, 'The Soldier tir'd of War's alarms', with trumpet accompaniment; Purcell's, 'Britons strike home', and Miller's, 'The Soldier's Adieu', which was a vocal version of his March for the 5th West Yorkshire Militia. Among the items in the second part was 'Britons ever shall be free', with words by the Duke of Leeds (see Chapter 11) and, for light relief, Miller's Glee, 'Variety' ('I'll live no more single'). This, which is only concerned with hostilities between man and wife, was published about 1800, with the heading, 'As sung at the Crown and Anchor Clubb'. The Crown and Anchor Tavern in the Strand, a favourite place for concerts, was for several years the meeting place of the Glee Club mentioned in the last chapter.

The second event was reported briefly in the 'Doncaster Gazette' of July 2nd 1802 -

'Mr. Brailsford's musical festival at Bradford this week, conducted by Dr. Miller of this town, was well attended; and the performances both at the church and concert room gave universal satisfaction.' The Mr. Brailsford mentioned above was the Doctor's natural son, Isaac, born in Doncaster in 1777 or 78. By 1802 he had become organist of Bradford, and in January of that year he married Nancy Willson of that town.

Perhaps Edward, realizing his age, had decided to 'take things a little easier', by refusing engagements at concerts or festivals. Such

THE MANSION HOUSE.
From Miller's 'History of Doncaster'.

events, often consisting of a major work in the morning, a miscellaneous concert in the evening, and perhaps rehearsals also, must have been exhausting both physically and mentally, and we are apt to forget in this age of motorways the difficulties of travel by coach, or on horseback, over the uncertain roads of two centuries ago. We receive no enlightenment from him on this, but he does tell us in the 'Gazette' that he had no intention of retiring from class music teaching -

'Dr. Miller, of Doncaster, respectfully informs his Friends, that having declined teaching in Mrs. Procter's School any longer, he is now at liberty to avail himself of their late kind applications. Church Hill, July 23rd 1799.'

This school, situated in South Parade, was directed by the Misses Procter, daughters of the Rev. Francis Procter, Vicar of Hatfield. In the preface to his 'Institutes of Music' Edward tells of his many years of employment as a music teacher in young ladies' Boarding Schools, but we do not know how long he was employed at the Misses Procter's, nor his reason for leaving that establishment. Some time in 1801 he became music master at Mr. Falconar's Classical, Commercial and Mathematical School for Young Gentlemen in Hallgate, a position he held until 1805. Doubtless he still had private pupils and we are reminded of this activity by a notice in the 'Gazette' of September 19th 1800, reporting the death of one of his more illustrious students, Francis Linley. Born in Doncaster in 1771 and blind from birth, Francis studied with Dr. Miller and eventually became organist of St. James' Chapel, Pentonville. He married a blind lady of considerable wealth and later purchased a music-selling business in Holborn. Difficulties both financial and domestic soon arose, his wife left him and he went to America where his playing and compositions were much admired. He returned to this country in 1799 and died at his mother's home in Doncaster on September 13th 1800 at the age of twenty-nine. His works include songs, pieces for the flute, pianoforte, and organ, and also an organ tutor which, by 1810, was in its tenth edition.

When we turn to Edward's music writing and publishing in the early years of the new century we find, not less, but greatly increased activity, giving the impression that there was still so much to be done and so little time in which to do it. Between 1800 and his death in 1807 he published at least six musical works, four of which were major publications, and also found time to produce a large and comprehensive history of the locality.

Most of his books, when they first appeared, were advertised in the 'York Courant' or the Doncaster paper, the notices being headed with the words, 'New Music published this day'. His Opera Ten, however, seems to have been an exception to the general rule, no advertisement for it having been found. This work of pleasing and varied songs for Soprano voice, some with parts for violin or flute, was given the title of 'Twelve Canzonets for the Voice and Pianoforte', and cost half a guinea (52½p). It was printed by Goulding, Phipps and D'Almaine of 45 Pall Mall, Music Sellers to Their Royal Highnesses the Prince and Princess of Wales, and a list of the composer's published and projected works, given on page two, suggests that it first appeared in 1799 or 1800. Two of the songs, 'Poor Little Rosalie' and 'The Primrose', are mentioned as having been sung by Miss Waters at the Theatre Royal, Covent Garden.

For some reason unknown, 'The New Flute Instructor' was never given an Opera number, but its arrival was announced in both the York and Doncaster papers of October and November, 1800. The firm of Broderip and Wilkinson, number 13, Haymarket, who printed it, came into being after the bankruptcy of Longman and Broderip in 1798. In his Introduction Edward says that the favourable reception given by the public to his 'Institutes of Music' had encouraged him to adopt the same plan for his new work, Part One being devoted to 'the Principles of Music inculcated by way of Question and Answer', and Part Two consisting of carefully graded solos, duets and trios for the instrument. Unlike the 'Institutes' however, 'The New Flute Instructor' was not intended for class study in the music room, while the teacher heard members perform individually, but solely for private tuition. After telling of his flute playing for Handel and his pioneering of 'double tongueing' in this country, both mentioned earlier in this book, he discusses 'that great essential of music called TIME'. He talks of brilliant performers who know so little of the principles of Time that they cannot play a simple tune at sight, and he condemns teachers who ignore this problem. He explains Time, and his method of counting the time, in great detail in Part One, following this up with carefully graded exercises in Part Two, exercises which have to be counted while being played. To many readers who have had practical experience of playing and counting - 'one and, two and, three and' - it may come as a surprise to learn that our author pioneered this teaching aid also -

'This method occurred to me by chance while teaching a lady. After repeated trials to have her turn . . . . . . four crotchets into eight quavers, and not being able to make her do them equally, as she always made the intermediate notes either too long or too short, I bethought myself to have her say "AND" . . . . thus, 1 and, 2 and, 3 and, 4 and, and on the very first trial she played the eight quavers in true and equal time.'

Another section deals with additional keys on the instrument. (See page 21).

Skill on a musical instrument, even with the guidance of an experienced teacher and the help of a good instruction book, has never been easy or quick to acquire. Edward was well aware of this and so one hopes that the publisher, and not the author, was responsible for the 'New Flute Instructor's' sub-title, 'The Art of playing the German Flute in a short time without the help of a Master'.

The same advertisements which introduced 'The New Flute Instructor' to the public also announced another new work by Miller, a volume of sacred music. After ten years of success with 'Psalms of David' it may have been expected that he would provide a further selection of metrical psalms and tunes for the Church of England, but this new collection was entirely different, containing not only metrical psalms but also 'human hymns' so disliked by authority, and intended for singers everywhere, including dissenters -

'DR. WATTS'S PSALMS AND HYMNS
Set to new music, consisting of upwards of
fifty original melodies or tunes, in three and
four parts, composed by
EDWARD MILLER, Mus. Doct.
To which is added a copious Appendix, containing the
most favourite Tunes now used in different congregations,
corrected and adapted to a new Selection of six hundred
hymns by the Rev. Dr. Williams and the Rev. Mr. Boden.
With reference to Dr. Watts.
This volume contains a greater variety than
any other extant, forming a publication of
near Three Hundred Tunes, an hundred of which
were never before printed; with words annexed -
the Basses figured, and the tunes not only
adapted for public worship, but also for private
use on the Organ or Piano Forte.
To which is added a short introduction to Psalmody,
with easy rules for singing. Published by Broderip
and Wilkinson, price ten shillings and sixpence.' (52½p)

More than a year before the above advertisement offered the book to the general public, proposals for printing a Subscription Edition appeared in the 'Gazette' of March 15th 1799. This special edition, in which a List of Subscribers would be printed, was promised for the July of the same year.

Thus the established church was gradually losing the fight. The hymn-writing eighteenth century, the century of Watts, the Wesleys, Cowper, Newton and others, was followed by a century or more of hymn singing in which 'human hymns' predominated, by far outnumbering the performances of metrical psalms. The sound of hymn singing coming from the meeting places and chapels of the dissenters, singing in which all could take part, attracted many to their midst, as William Edward had been drawn to the chapel in Norfolk Street, Sheffield. More and more hymns were written and many an amateur instrumentalist, with little or no knowledge of composition, aspired to provide music for them, no doubt encouraged, but often deceived, by the apparent simplicity of the task.

Dr. Miller must have realized that his 'Psalms of David', in spite of being a successful and widely used publication, was rapidly becoming too limited in its appeal. Its total reliance on the metrical psalm meant that before long, even in many Anglican churches, it would be outdated. There was a growing need for a book which contained both metrical psalms and 'human hymns', in which the well-loved and generally staid tunes of past centuries were joined by more florid airs favoured by many nonconformists, a book in fact which would appeal to Anglican and Dissenter alike. Just how he came to collaborate with the Rev. Dr. Williams is not known, but they must have been well acquainted, for in his Last Will and Testament he appointed his dear friend, the Rev. Edward Williams, Doctor in Divinity, as one of his executors. For the last eighteen years of his life the Reverend Doctor was Principal Tutor at the Independent Academy at Rotherham and also Pastor of Masborough Independent Chapel. On September 17th 1800 he took part in an Ordination Service at the small Independent Chapel in Hallgate, Doncaster, which was known as Ebenezer Chapel, and when a new Independent Chapel was built almost on the same site, (the present United Reformed Church), he preached at the opening service on October 17th 1804. When he died in 1813 he was buried in a vault under the pulpit in Masborough Chapel, and the Rev. James Boden, Pastor of Queen Street Independent Chapel, Sheffield, conducted the funeral service.

Towards the end of the eighteenth century Dr. Williams was engaged in the compiling and editing of two different hymn books. The first was to be an improved edition of the psalms and hymns of Isaac Watts, who was at one time Pastor of the Independent Congregation in Mark Lane, London. There had been many editions of Watts's works from the 1720's onwards, but according to Dr. Williams, most were shamefully inaccurate or poorly printed, hence his desire to produce a volume worthy of the poet. About the year 1799 'The Psalms and Hymns of Dr. Watts', by Edward Williams D.D. was printed in Doncaster by D. Boys, opposite the Cross in the Market Place, and Dr. Miller wrote 'upwards of fifty original melodies or tunes, in three or four parts', for use with it.

In his other book, 'A Collection of above Six Hundred Hymns designed as a New Supplement to Dr. Watts's Psalms and Hymns', Dr. Williams collaborated with his fellow minister, the Rev. James Boden. It was stressed in the Foreword that this was not intended to supersede the work of Dr. Watts, but to complement it, by including hymns written during the century by the Wesleys, Doddridge, Toplady, Newton and others, together with some hymns never previously published. It was for this collection, also printed by D. Boys in Doncaster, that Dr. Miller selected about two hundred tunes, new and old, which made up his 'copious Appendix'. The two collections of hymns, published in separate volumes, and the music for both, which was issued in one book as shown in the above advertisement, were all planned to appear simultaneously.

The title page of Edward's combined volume has a familiar look, for the vignette which had been used in 'Psalms of David' appears again, no doubt for reasons of economy. In the Foreword, which he preferred to call 'Advertisement', he criticised the music written by others for the hymns and psalms of Dr. Watts just as his collaborators had expressed dissatisfaction with other editions of the words -

'It is true, that a very slight knowledge in music, with the assistance of a good ear, may enable a person to make a pretty melody or treble; but he should make farther advances in the science before he venture to publish music in parts . . . . .'

His own 'upwards of fifty original melodies or tunes in three or four parts', were all named after Reformers, Martyrs and eminent Divines, Calvin and Cranmer rubbing shoulders with Luther and Latimer, and Watts himself being similarly honoured. Liberally sprinkled with quavers and semiquavers, pitched rather high, and in a style more florid than that of 'Psalms of David', Edward was obviously writing with the enthusiastic and fervent singing of dissenters in mind. All these tunes have long been forgotten.

His 'copious Appendix' comes next, and this had its own title-page -

'Sacred Music
containing 250 of the most favourite tunes
now commonly sung at the Churches, Chapels
and Dissenting Meetings in England and Ireland
and also in the Protestant Churches and Chapels
abroad . . . . . . adapted to a New Selection of Hymns by
the Rev. Mr. Boden and Dr. Williams, the music
selected for 2, 3 and 4 voices by Edward Miller,
Mus.Doct.'

His selection was both wide and good. Many well-established tunes
were included (e.g. 'Adeste Fideles'; Carey's 'Easter Hymn'; 'Hanover';
'Irish' and 'Wareham'), a few of which, ('St. Ann(e)' and 'Old
Hundredth' for example), had appeared in 'Psalms of David'. Alongside
these were comparative newcomers which are now firm favourites (e.g.
'Darwall's 148th'; 'Leoni'; Shrubsole's 'Miles Lane' and 'Warrington'),
and others like 'Simeon', which after a long period of great popularity,
particularly among dissenters, are rarely heard today. There were tunes
too which had not been previously published, including some by Edward
and his son William Edward, and one tune appearing for the first time in
any hymn book, which was to become famous. Haydn's 'Hymn to the
Emperor' was first performed on the Emperor's birthday, February 12th
1797. The 'Musical Times' states that Burney introduced it into this
country with the words translated, but it was in this collection of Miller's
that it first appeared as an ordinary hymn tune. He called it 'Haydn' and
used it as a 7.7.7.7. Double metre, the words beginning, 'Jesu, soft
harmonious name, Ev'ry faithful heart's desire'. These words and the
tune were uncomfortable together - the same effect is obtained if it is
sung to the words of 'Jesu, lover of my soul' - but by 1809 the tune had
become an 8.7.8.7. Double metre, to the well-known 'Praise the Lord, ye
heav'ns adore Him'. Now generally called 'Austria', it was a great
favourite of the composer's. He created it from a Croatian melody he
knew as a child, and used it again as the basis of a set of variations in the
'Emperor Quartet'. It was the last tune he ever played. From 1797 until
the Republic was set up in 1918 it was the Austrian National Anthem,
and with new words, it is still popular in that country today. It is also the
National Anthem of the West German Federal Republic.

When hymn books were in their infancy it was quite common for a
tune to appear in different books under different names. J. T. Lightwood
in 'Hymn-Tunes and their story' (Kelly, 1905) tells what happened to
John Wainwright's well-known tune for 'Christians Awake'. This was
first known as 'Mortram' (Mottram?), but when Wainwright himself
published a collection of tunes it was printed unnamed. A few years later
it was known as 'Stockport', and in America it became 'Walworth' or

'Wolworth'. In England at different times it was 'Leamington', 'Dorchester', 'Wainwright', 'Nativity', 'Bethlehem', 'Longtown' and 'Yorkshire', and it is by this last name that it is known today. Why it became 'Yorkshire' is a mystery, for Wainwright was born at Stockport in Cheshire. There are tunes which suffered changes of name in Miller's collection too, but only their present-day names are used here. It was common also, no doubt due to ignorance, to attribute tunes to the wrong composer.

On April 12th 1805 the 'Gazette' advertised a Second Edition of Miller's tune-book, and on September 27th of the same year - a few weeks before Nelson's victory at Trafalgar - it announced publication of a second volume, from which time the original work was known as Volume One. In Volume Two all his original tunes to Dr. Watts's 'Psalms and Hymns' were in four parts, and he provided a new selection of tunes for 'Sacred Music', bringing the total number of tunes in both volumes to four hundred and seventy. Ten additional pieces for the practice of Societies of Singers were also given in the second volume, together with some favourite Airs and Duets 'for the domestic use at the Piano Forte on a Sunday Evening'. A second edition of the second volume appeared at the end of 1806.

One wonders what influence any one book of hymns and tunes, published early in the nineteenth century, had on the large number of similar works which followed. J. T. Lightwood seems to have had no doubt in Miller's case, for after mentioning only two other tune books of that period in his 'Hymn-Tunes and their Story' (Kelly, 1905), he has this to say -

'It is unnecessary to examine in further detail the contents of the various tune-books issued during the first forty years of the century. They were all more or less reproductions of Miller's edition of Watts'.

It is interesting to note that round about the time Edward's second volume of 'Dr. Watts's Psalms and Hymns' appeared, his son William Edward was editing 'David's Harp'. This was a collection of about three hundred tunes adapted to Mr. Wesley's selection of hymns, one hundred of those tunes having been expressly composed for the work by William Edward and his father. 'W.E.' hoped that it would become the standard book of the Methodist Society, and to some extent this hope was realized, for J. T. Lightwood describes it as the most important Methodist tune-book between 1789 and 1876.

Only two more works of Edward Miller, together with some mention of his sheet music, remain to be considered, for it is intended to give his 'History of Doncaster' a chapter of its own. The 'Doncaster

Gazette' advertisement of April 12th 1805, which has already been mentioned, told also of the publication that day of 'An Anthem performed on a Commencement at St. Mary's Church, Cambridge, to which is added a Hymn for Sunday Schools and Schools of Industry'. This was published by W. Sheardown at the 'Gazette' office in Doncaster, price seven shillings and sixpence (37½p), and parts for a Full Band could be obtained separately. Nothing is known of this work, no copy having been found, but the title suggests that the anthem was written for the Commencement mentioned in Chapter seven at which Miller was admitted a Doctor of Music. (See page 53).

Only a few months before his death a notice in the 'Gazette' (July 17th 1807) announced the publication of 'A Musical Primer', dedicated to all those parents who have children learning music, and intended as a Companion to 'Institutes of Music'. Again, no copy has been found, but title, sub-title and the price, which was half a crown (12½p), suggest that it was a supplementary book or booklet throwing further light on some aspect of musical rudiments.

The term 'Sheet Music' is used here to describe Edward's secular vocal compositions which do not appear in his three song-books (See Chapters 2, 4 and 12), and which were either published as separate pieces or never published at all. We have already seen that he provided music for poems celebrating local events, including the visit of the Prince of Wales to Wentworth and the procession in honour of Bishop Blaize at Doncaster. International events also did not go unsung, for we have told of his song to words by the Duke of Leeds at the Sheffield Festival of 1794, his song on the execution of the Queen of France, a vocal arrangement called 'War and Justice' for the Yorkshire Cavalry and Sheffield Volunteers, and a vocal version of his march for the Fifth West Yorkshire Militia entitled 'Britons strike home'. Another of his settings which reflected that unsettled age was 'The Little French Emigrée', sung by Mrs. McGeorge, the author of the words, at Bury St. Edmunds on Friday, July 27th 1798 ('Bury and Norwich Post'). Quite often, in reporting concerts at which these items were performed, the local periodical printed the words of the songs in full, but unfortunately the music, which was probably in manuscript, has been lost. The music for only one of the above items is known to exist, a copy of 'Britons ever shall be free', with words by the Duke of Leeds, and arranged for a Military Band by Edward Miller, can be seen in the British Library. Another of his songs which refers to a burning issue of the last decade of the eighteenth century is 'The Negro Boy, who was sold by an African Prince for a Metal Watch. A Favorite Song, Sung by Mr. Burrows, at the Public Concerts'. This was printed for J. Dale, No. 19, Cornhill, and No. 132, Oxford Street, a well-known musician, musical instrument maker and

VIEW OF FRENCHGATE AND HIGH STREET, DONCASTER.
From Friars' Bridge c. 1802.

publisher, who occupied those premises from 1791 to about 1802. Its price was one shilling (5p), and there is a copy in the University Library, Cambridge. The remorse shown by the Prince in this song echoed the growing agitation in this country against the trading in slaves -

> *'In Isles that deck the western main*
> *Th'unhappy Youth was doomed to dwell,*
> *A poor, forlorn, insulted Slave,*
> *A Beast, that Christians buy and sell;*
> *And yet for this same, simple Toy,*
> *I sold the weeping Negro Boy.'*

Amid a growing feeling of horror at this trade in human beings a society for its suppression was founded in 1787 by Thomas Clarkson and William Wilberforce, and it is interesting to note that the Rev. William Mason (Ch. 4) was an early anti-slavery agitator and preached a sermon on this subject in York Minster on January 27th 1788. A Bill for the abolition of this trade was rejected in 1789, the parliamentary preoccupation with the French Wars tending to push this issue into the background, but in 1807 the slave trade was made illegal by Act of Parliament. Clarkson and Wilberforce turned next to the emancipation of existing slaves, and three days before he died in 1833, Wilberforce was informed that Parliament had passed a Bill which ended slavery in our colonies.

Three more songs by Edward, at least two of which appear to have been of a topical nature, were advertised by Longman and Broderip in the 'York Courant' during November and December, 1790 -

'Ye Britons Bold'.   1s. 0d. (5p)
'I'm monarch of all I survey'   6d. (2½p)
'The Afflicted African'   1s. 6d. (7½p)

No copies of these are known.

Unlike the sheet music mentioned above, his three song-books forgot the world and its troubles and told of young lovers, nymphs and shepherds, primroses and glistening dewdrops, sleep and ghosts, only coming down to earth occasionally to lament the passing of Handel, or to listen to the unfortunate Mary, Queen of Scots. They were songs to charm and delight at Vauxhall and Covent Gardens as well as at concert halls in provincial towns and cities. In 1937 four of the songs from his song-books were published by Boosey and Company, with accompaniments which, while retaining their eighteenth-century flavour, were more suited to twentieth-century audiences. They were the work of Dr. Cecil Armstrong Gibbs, who had been introduced to them by Mrs. George Bramwell of Baughurst, near Basingstoke, a great, great, granddaughter of Edward Miller. (See Ch. 14.)

Two more non-topical songs by Miller appeared in the 'Lady's Musical Magazine' of November, 1788 -

'Fair Sophia', with words by Horace Walpole, and 'Serious Epigram', with words by Sir William Jones.

We met Sir William, Judge of the High Court at Calcutta, in Chapter Eleven. Was Edward's setting of his words the 'Morceau delicat' of William Edward's letter from India to his father in 1790?

Chapter Thirteen

On the first day of October in the year 1802, a long and detailed advertisement in the 'Doncaster Gazette' informed the readers that Dr. Miller proposed to publish a 'History of Doncaster and the adjacent towns and villages'. This, the first History of the town, was to be 'handsomely printed in Quarto' and 'embellished with Elegant Engravings.... from the most interesting Subjects, executed by eminent Artists'. Particulars were also given of the dealers who would be pleased to take names of intending subscribers, and the advertisement concluded by giving a list of those who had already subscribed, a list in which the Nobility was represented by the Duke of Leeds, Earls Fitzwilliam and Scarbrough, and Lords Milton, Harewood, Downe, and Galway. Parliamentary subscribers included the two Yorkshire members, the Hon. H. Lascelles and the Hon. William Wilberforce, and among the local gentry were the names of Sir George Cooke, Bart., George Cooke Yarborough Esq., and Thomas Copley Esq. When this advertisement next appeared, on October 22nd, the King's name headed a further list, the footnote stating that 'His Majesty has been graciously pleased to direct his Name to be placed at the Head of the Subscribers to Dr. Miller's "History of Doncaster and its vicinity"'. No further reference to the book was made until May 13th of the following year, when the 'Gazette' carried this request -

'Doctor Miller presents his best respects to those Clergymen of such parts of the Deanery of Doncaster whose livings are situated between Rotherham to the West, and Pontefract to the North of Doncaster; and he will be very thankful for the communication of the inscription of any remarkable Monument in their respective churches; with the Date of the year when their parish register commenced, or any other interesting particulars with which they may honour him, before or at the Visitation at Doncaster, on Friday the 10th day of June 1803.'

More than a year elapsed before the 'History' was mentioned again, and then, on September 21st 1804, the 'Gazette's' readers were informed that -

'The Corporation of Doncaster, at a Meeting on Monday last, presented Dr. Miller with £50 for his "History of Doncaster and its Vicinity", which will be published in a few days'.

The few days became a few weeks, for it was not until November 9th that the paper reported the book to be ready at the publishers, price one guinea in Boards (£1.05p),with a few copies on fine paper at one guinea and a half. (£1.57½p)

The full title of the work is 'The History and Antiquities of Doncaster and its Vicinity, with Anecdotes of Eminent Men'. A detailed map of the area, about a square foot in size when unfolded, faces the title page. Next comes the Dedication - 'To the Worshipful the Mayor and Corporation of the Ancient Borough and Soke of Doncaster' - followed by the names of more than five hundred subscribers, who had ordered more than five hundred and sixty copies. The author, after thanking his learned friends in the neighbourhood for their assistance, emphasizes in the Introduction that he 'has not been satisfied with mere verbal intelligence, nor relied entirely on the kind communications of friends; but has also found it necessary to visit every church, town and village, of which he has given a description'.

It is a matter for speculation why Dr. Miller, when in his late sixties, put his music writing on one side for a few years and turned to the immense task of producing a four hundred Quarto-page history of Doncaster. Nothing in his previous writings and activities suggests any particular interest in the history and antiquities in his adopted town and its surroundings. We are given the impression that his non-musical pursuits were chiefly of a financial nature, concerned with the letting of property, the selling of sand and some small-scale farming. Moreover, the writing of a lengthy volume was quite new to him, his previous works being chiefly in musical notation or in the form of short pamphlets. Nevertheless, after the year 1800 his music publications ceased for a few years, his time no doubt being fully occupied by what he describes in the Introduction as 'the zeal in inquiry', the 'labor in procuring', and the 'drudgery of compiling'.

It is not proposed to give a detailed account of the 'History', for those sufficiently interested will not find much difficulty in seeing a Library copy. Before considering the sources of the Doctor's material, however, the following short summary should be sufficient to indicate the comprehensive nature of his undertaking.

The first half of the book, consisting of nine chapters or 'Sections', as Miller preferred to describe them, is devoted to the town and neighbourhood. A brief account of the West Riding, with a more detailed picture of the Don Valley, is followed by sections on natural history and the general state of agriculture. In Sections four and five we are introduced to the history of the town from its days as a Roman station to the account by Leland of his visit in the 1530's. Two relics, the Roman Votive Altar found in St. Sepulchre Gate in 1781, and the twelfth-century Doncaster Cross, a so-called replica of which still exists, are illustrated and described in detail. Section six tells of charters, fairs and grants, important visitors, and local events recalling the Wars of the Roses, the Pilgrimage of Grace, the Dissolution of the Monasteries, the Commonwealth and the Restoration. Law proceedings, taxes, fines and rates relating to the ancient state of the town are also set out. The forty pages in the seventh section are concerned with the church and its antiquities, its monuments and stained glass, the organ and belfry, the church plate and other furnishings. We read of the 'lending library' of about four hundred volumes in the room over the porch, and the author's account of the 'psalmody of the church', which we quoted in chapter nine, is also found in this section. Present-day readers will find the pages on the church fabric and its history both vague and disappointing, until it is realised that little was known of Gothic architecture at that time. The Liverpool architect, Thomas Rickman, was the first person to write authoritatively on the subject, and his book, 'An Attempt to Discriminate the Styles of Architecture in England', did not appear until 1817. This work went through many editions and profoundly influenced subsequent writers. Rickman was the first to divide Gothic architecture into the three periods, Early English, Decorated and Perpendicular. Section eight gives memoirs of eminent men born in and around Doncaster, and the final section in the first part of the book describes the state of the town at the beginning of the nineteenth century, from its buildings, which included chapels, almshouse, poor-house, theatre and Dispensary, to its manufactories, markets, Sunday schools, sick-clubs and races. Many of the 'History's' references to music have already been noted.

More than ninety towns, villages and hamlets within ten or twelve miles of Doncaster are described in the second part of the work. Detailed accounts are presented of the castles, abbeys and churches in the area, the seats of the nobility and gentry, with particulars of the local markets and fairs, agriculture and industries. We learn of Rotherham's iron-works, Wickersley's grindstones, Greasbrough's many collieries, the 'raddle' mines of Micklebring and the quarries at Hooton Roberts, from which the stone for the building of Wentworth House was obtained. The church at Thorne possessed a barrel organ, we are told, but the church at Scrooby was 'dirty and indecent'. The pages are peopled too, the stories including the slaying at Hatfield of Edwin, first Christian King of Northumbria, the search for the Royalist Major Portington at Arksey during Commonwealth days, George Fox's encounter with troops when preaching at Balby, and the highwayman Nevison's armed robbery at Woodlands.

The accounts vary considerably in length, from Auckley's line and a half - 'this village contains nothing remarkable' - to fourteen pages on Conisbrough, with its castle and church. Brevity was not necessarily due to the lack of interesting features, but partly to the poor response by some of the clergy. 'Had the assistance of this reverend body been more general', the Doctor complains, 'this history, of course, would have been more worthy the patronage of the public'. Writing of Hooton Roberts he says, 'After several applications, I have not been able to obtain a copy of the date when this church register commences'. Of the church at Thurnscoe he tells us that he also made several applications for information, but unfortunately without success.

Part Two closes with Doctor Miller asking for pardon for the many defects which may be discovered in his work, written as it was, 'under the pressure of declining years, and increasing infirmities'. It is interesting to note that when writing of Askern he was actually staying there and taking the medicinal waters for the benefit of his health.

The 'History' ends with a forty-five page Appendix in which the nine existing Royal Charters of the Corporation of Doncaster were printed for the first time in English, together with other private Grants, Petitions and Decrees extracted from the Records. Unfortunately, three other Royal Charters, those of Henry VII, Edward VI and James I had disappeared.

In Volume Four of the 'Calendar of the Records of Doncaster', p. 242, dated September 26th 1771, is the following entry -
'Ordered that Mr. Richard Tetlow be paid 75 guineas (£78.75p) and a cup valued 10 guineas (£10.50p), with the Corporation's Arms engraved thereon, for transcribing and translating the several charters of the Corporation. Also ordered that copies of the translation be bound.'

Richard John Tetlow was a well-known antiquary living at Ferrybridge, and it was his translation of the nine Royal Charters, dating from that of Richard I (May 22nd 1194), to the second Charter of James II (November 10th 1688) that Dr. Miller used. No subsequent writer has included them for, as Joseph Hunter says in his 'South Yorkshire' (1828) -
'The work of Dr. Miller, which was published in 1804, has rendered it unnecessary to introduce into this volume copies of the Charters, and a list of the chief magistrates of Doncaster. There are also other things which might have found a place here, had they not already been communicated to the public in his work'.

In addition to a number of small illustrations found throughout the book, ten full-page engravings present a valuable record of the main buildings in the town and its neighbourhood nearly two centuries ago.

In preparing his 'History' the Doctor was fortunate in having the assistance of a few knowledgeable friends who lived near by, the help of most of the clergy in the Deanery, and access to a large number of works by authorities on various aspects of South Yorkshire. In the Introduction he thanks his friends Edwood Chorley, Robert Wylde Moult and Joseph Hunter for 'their liberal communications'. Edwood Chorley, M.D. was born in the 1750's, became Mayor of Doncaster in 1821-2 and was at one time a Captain in the Doncaster Troop of the South West Yorkshire Yeomanry Cavalry. He was physician to the Doncaster Dispensary when it opened in 1792, and an authority on the natural history of the area. He died in 1831. Robert Wylde Moult (c.1749-1810), local historian and genealogist, lived the life of a country gentleman at Wickersley, near Rotherham. Both his father, the Rev. Samuel Moult, and his grandfather the Rev. William Moult were dissenting ministers, his grandfather marrying the daughter of the Rev. Samuel Crompton, who was a dissenting minister in Doncaster. Moult was a friend of the antiquarian, Joseph Hunter of Sheffield (1783-1861). In 1809 Hunter was a dissenting minister in Bath, and in 1833 he became a Sub-Commissioner of Public Records, later becoming Assistant Keeper. His 'History of Hallamshire' appeared in 1819, and his 'South Yorkshire' in 1828. Miller also mentioned the great help he had from William Radclyffe Esq., Rouge Croix Pursuivant of Arms in the College of Heralds. Though he complained of the lack of response from certain of the clergy there is no doubt that the majority helped him to the best of their ability. He asked them particularly for information concerning the church registers, and in only a small minority of instances was this information withheld.

When we think of the last decades of the eighteenth century, with the postal system in its infancy, travel slow and often difficult, the telephone unknown, and public libraries non-existent, we cannot but marvel at the numerous and varied sources at the Doctor's disposal. These ranged from Leland's 'Antiquities' of the sixteenth century; Camden's 'Britannia' of the century following; Drake's 'Eboracum', Burton's 'Monasticon' and Gough's 'Topography' of the eighteenth century; to works almost contemporary with the 'History' itself, including Robert Brown's, 'View of the Agriculture of the West Riding of Yorkshire' (1799). No doubt some of the books he used were on his own shelves or the shelves of his friends, and it is possible that he also had entry to libraries in one or more of the great houses of the district, for in Section Eight he thanks Lord Galway of Serlby for allowing him to copy from a manuscript in his possession.

More important, however, than the knowledge which came from the spoken or written words of others, was the recording of the author's own observations made during a long life in the area, his eye-witness accounts of the changing face of the countryside, the appearance of the towns and villages of two centuries ago, and the workaday life and leisure pursuits of the inhabitants. Joseph Hunter realised this, for in his 'South Yorkshire', published only twenty-four years after Miller's 'History', he says - '.....my late friend Dr. Edward Miller, a man highly accomplished in his own profession, and whose "History of Doncaster", the work of his old age, is best in the parts in which he depended on himself, and was not encumbered with the communications of his antiquarian friends.....'

Today, when viewed from a distance of almost two hundred years, Miller's observations assume a much greater importance.

Quite possibly there could have been not one, but two different Histories of Doncaster, for Hunter has this to say of the Rev. George Hay Drummond, Miller's collaborator in 'Psalms of David' -

'at one period of his life (he) seriously meditated to undertake the History of Doncaster and some places in its vicinity, particularly those in which the estates of the Kinnoul family lay. A man of his elegant turn of mind could not but have produced an agreeable work. He relinquished the undertaking, leaving what he had collected in a large portfolio. This portfolio, his son, Mr. Hay, has entrusted to me in a most gratifying manner, and I have received much useful assistance from the notes and references it contains.'

The contents of this portfolio are now in the library of the Yorkshire Archaeological Society, Leeds. (MS 387).

Chapter Fourteen

'On Saturday evening September the 12th, died after an illness of two months Dr. Miller, well known in the Musical and Literary Circles as a man of genius and integrity'.

Thus began a report in the 'Doncaster Gazette' of Friday, September 18th 1807, which, after outlining the Doctor's career and making special mention of his music for both the established church and dissenting congregations, concluded with the following paragraph -

'After a long life actively spent in the hurry and dissipation of general society, he gradually retired from the busy hum of men, and in the company of a few religious friends sought for that acceptance with God, which he knew could only be obtained by a saving faith in the atonement of Jesus Christ. In humble and trembling hope he entered into the unknown world, and his last end was peace.
He was 75 years of age, and was upwards of 50 years Organist at this place'.

He was in fact, only 71, and the 'York Courant' of September 21st, also gave the age incorrectly -

'On Saturday se'nnight died, in the 76th year of his age, Dr. Edward Miller, 51 years Organist of Doncaster'.

This error of believing him to have been born in 1731 is perpetuated in the 'Dictionary of National Biography' and Grove's 'Dictionary of Music and Musicians' (5th Edition), but the registers of St. Peter Mancroft, Norwich, show clearly that the eldest son Thomas, who became the 'Bungay Bookseller', was born in 1731, and Edward four years later. The report in the 'Courant', after describing the Doctor as 'the father of the profession in the North of England', singles out his 'Elements of Thorough Bass and Composition' (Op. 5) for special praise -
'In this book science, simplicity and practice are happily united, forming the first work of its kind'.

His Last Will and Testament, from which the following items are extracted, was made on December 16th 1802 -

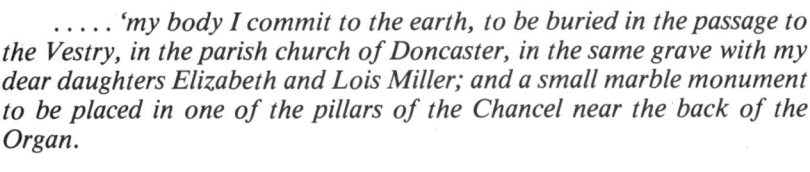

..... 'my body I commit to the earth, to be buried in the passage to the Vestry, in the parish church of Doncaster, in the same grave with my dear daughters Elizabeth and Lois Miller; and a small marble monument to be placed in one of the pillars of the Chancel near the back of the Organ.

..... I constitute and appoint my dear Son William Edward Miller and my dear friends the reverend Edward Williams, Doctor in Divinity, and George Cooke Yarborough Esquire jointly Executors of this my Last Will and Testament, requesting each of them to accept of a Ring as a small token of my gratitude.

..... I give and bequeath to my dear wife Margaret Miller, an Annuity for life of seventy pounds p.annum, to be paid her by two equal half-yearly payments, from the rental of my estate in the Sand Closes in Wheatley and from the produce of my mortgages on the estates of Thomas Copley Esq., and of Robert Chester, Taylor, both of Doncaster aforesaid.

..... All my household furniture, musical instruments and books to be sold, from which sum my debts and funeral expenses to be discharged, in lieu of which, my Wife, Margaret to have the sum of one hundred pounds and also to have my Harpsichord or Piano Forte, and, if she chuses it, my picture by Wright. (See Appendix Eight).

..... after the decease of my said Wife, I give and bequeath to Isaac Brailsford, the present Organist of Bradford, and to his heirs and assigns the sum of three hundred pounds, and to his brother Edward Brailsford his heirs and assigns, the sum of three hundred pounds, to be paid out of the money of my Wife's life annuity within six months after her decease, and the remainder of all my property, I give and bequeath to my son William Edward Miller and his heirs.

..... In consideration of the expense and trouble the reverend Dr. Edward Williams has had in procuring melodies and words for the two volumes of Dr. Watts' Psalms and hymns, with the supplement published by me; at my decease he, his heirs and assigns, shall have the liberty of purchasing the plates and copyright of the said two volumes at a sum not exceeding forty pounds.' (Borthwick Institute)

On September 19th 1807, George Cooke Yarborough legally renounced his executorship for 'divers good Causes and Considerations' which were not given. (Borthwick Institute). He was seventy years of age and had known Edward from the time when both were members of the

Nether Hall music group some fifty years before. His renunciation explains why only two executors are mentioned in the 'Gazette' notice of September 25th. Headed 'Debtors and Creditors' it requested those to whom Edward was indebted at the time of his death to send an account of their demands against him to William Edward Miller of Rochdale, Edward Williams near Rotherham, or Thomas Brooke, Solicitor of Doncaster. On the other hand, all persons who stood indebted to the deceased were requested to pay their debts forthwith.

Presumably the burial on the 17th of September, 'in the passage to the Vestry,' was in the North Chapel, for the plan in the Rev. J. E. Jackson's 'History and Description of St. George's Church at Doncaster' (1855), shows a vestry in its north-east corner. The position of the 'small marble monument to be placed in one of the pillars of the Chancel near the back of the Organ', can be more readily pictured when it is recalled that the instrument stood in a loft at the tower crossing and was thus between nave and chancel.

The inscription on the marble appears to have been the work of William Edward, the family's sole survivor -

'In Memory
of Elizabeth, wife of Edward Miller,
Doctor in Music.
She was born August 8th, 1745;
she died August 14th, 1773.
Also of her three daughters
Elizabeth, Mary, and Lois
And of her third son
Thomas, a midshipman, who was shipwrecked
in the "Halsewell" on the rocks of Purbeck.
These children all died in the bloom of youth.
Also EDWARD MILLER, Mus. D.,
who died Sept. 13th, 1807, aged 72 years;
nearly 52 years Organist of this Church;
author of "Improvement in Psalmody"
"History of Doncaster", &c. &c.
After having served the world for many years,
at last he strove to serve his God;
and there is hope that, by sincere repentance
and a lively faith
in the crucified Redeemer, he died in peace.

Farewell, farewell, ye much-loved kindred dust!
One mourner's left to rear the votive bust;
But soon conjoined we'll hail the happy shore,
And mingling souls again will part no more!'

(Noted in Jackson's 'History and Description of St. George's Church at Doncaster' p. 95).

It will be seen that the children who died in infancy are not mentioned, and Edward's age is still not quite correct and even the date of his death is wrong. He was certainly in his seventy-second year but not seventy-two.

This Miller memorial, and the organ Edward had played for so long, are no more with us, for in the early morning of February 28th 1853, St. George's was totally destroyed by fire, the only items saved being the Church Plate, and the Parish Registers, some of which were badly damaged. The monumental brasses withstood the flames and were found afterwards amongst the ruins. An eyewitness, Joseph Clark, tanner of Frenchgate, writing to a relative, told of being roused on a beautiful, clear, frosty morning and seeing that all within the church was one vivid red glow. As wall, or roof, or bell fell into the wreck below an increasing stream of glowing embers shot up into the heavens. He continued - 'At four the fire had done its worst, I went to take some rest till six, when I went to the yard; when I returned at eight I hoped the tower, although gutted would stand, as I was assured it was safe, and this would have been a happy circumstance; but as I was choosing my road across, which was partly stopped up by rubbish and by the police, I heard a crash, looked round - the fine old tower, splitting from top to bottom, fell a shapeless mass; one side of it stood till evening, when this again rent its whole height, leaving the corner containing the belfry steps still braving the fury of the elements. . . . .'

Exactly one year later, on February 28th 1854, the foundation stone of the present church was laid on the same site by Thomas Musgrave, D.D., Lord Archbishop of York, and on October 14th 1858, the new church was consecrated. The architect was George Gilbert Scott. The present organ, by Schulze, was installed in 1862.

Before leaving the last Will and Testament some mention must be made of Mrs. Miller's annuity, the picture by Mr. Wright, and the Doctor's immediate descendants.

RUINS OF ST. GEORGE'S CHURCH, DONCASTER.
Destroyed by fire, 28th February 1853.

Thomas Copley was in grave financial difficulty during the latter part of his life and spent some time as a debtor in the King's Bench Prison, London. In 1801, after taking up residence at Carr Grange, the house built by Miller near his smallholding, he advertised Nether Hall, with its gardens, pleasure-grounds, paddocks, stables, coach-houses, granaries and other suitable offices, to be let furnished. (Doncaster Gazette, May 1st). It is known that he bought Carr Grange from Edward, and probably the mortgage mentioned in the Will was connected with that transaction.

The other mortgage concerned £300 borrowed by the tailor, Robert Chester, on the strength of his property in Goose Hill. There was still £200 of this owing when it was redeemed in 1809 (Doncaster Archives, Box D3).

Edward's second wife Margaret died in the neighbourhood of London on May 28th 1838, after being widowed for more than thirty years. After her death the two Brailsfords were each to receive £300 before the remainder of the estate passed to William Edward. Isaac, no doubt, received his share, but Edward Brailsford had died in 1822 at the age of 36, and his inheritance would pass to his son, Charles James. A year after Margaret's death William Edward disposed of the Sand Closes in Wheatley to John Silvester. (Sheffield City Library). It is not known whether Dr. Williams bought the copyright and engraved plates of 'Dr. Watts's Psalms and Hymns', or whether Mrs. Miller decided to keep the portrait by Wright of Derby.

Joseph Wright was born in Derby in 1734, the youngest son of John Wright, attorney. In 1751 his father sent him to London where he studied for two years with Thomas Hudson, who was also the master of Joshua Reynolds. Returning to his native town he commenced portrait painting, but he had a further period of study with Hudson about 1756. He was noted for his employment of strong effects of light and shade, often using the light of a candle to illuminate his figures. He was an accomplished musician too, and his Account Book records the purchase of a German Flute. In 1773 he made a lengthy visit to Italy and many of the pictures which he later exhibited at the Royal Academy were of Italian scenes. His only known portrait painting journey took place between 1760 and 1762 when he visited Retford, Lincoln, Newark, Boston, Thorne and Doncaster. (See Benedict Nicolson's 'Joseph Wright of Derby - Painter of Light', Routledge and Kegan Paul, 1968. Two Vols.). His Doncaster clients included William Brooke, several times mayor, Mr. and Mrs. Pigot, and Edward Miller. William Pigot was the son of the Vicar of Doncaster, and his wife was Brooke's daughter.

Miller's portrait, which was probably quite small and perhaps only head and shoulders, was no doubt a youthful one, for he was still in his middle twenties and not married. Since being mentioned in the Last Will and Testament nothing further has been heard of this picture.

Miller also sat to Thomas Hardy of London, a portrait painter of repute and a contemporary of Wright. This work has also disappeared but fortunately, engravings taken from it by the artist himself are still with us. Hardy exhibited thirty-one portraits at the Academy between 1778 and 1798, the subjects including Mr. Salomon the violinist, and Mr. Haydn the composer, both in 1792; Portrait of a Gentleman, and Mr. Cramer the violinist, both in 1794; and Dr. Arnold in 1796. (See 'The Royal Academy of Arts. 1769-1904.' by Algernon Graves, F.S.A.). One wonders whether Miller was the subject of 'Portrait of a Gentleman'. Some of these portraits were engraved and at least two of them (Mr. Cramer and Mr. Salomon) were published by John Bland, engraver, printer, music publisher and seller, of 45, High Holborn. It was this John Bland who was commissioned to visit Vienna in 1787 in order to invite Haydn to come to England, and when the composer did arrive in 1791, he was Bland's guest for a short time. Bland was succeeded in 1795 by Lewis, Houston and Hyde who, in March 1797, advertised the business for sale, together with about twelve thousand engraved plates. The purchaser was Francis Linley, the blind organist, who in the following year sold the business to William Hodsoll. (See 'Music Publishing in the British Isles, from the earliest times to the middle of the nineteenth century', Humphries and Smith. Cassell. 1954).

In 'The Connoisseur' of January 1935, a letter was published from Mrs. George Bramwell, whom we have already mentioned, seeking information concerning the whereabouts of the portrait of Dr. Miller which was painted and engraved by T. Hardy, and according to Mrs. Bramwell, was published in 1796 by F. Linley. She enclosed a copy of the engraving, which was published with her letter, but it appears that her query went unanswered, for there is no reply in any of the issues of 1935 and 1936.

The Rev. J. E. Jackson, in his 'History and Description of St. George's Church at Doncaster' (p. 59), states that, 'the portrait of him by T. Hardy, from which the engraving by the same artist was taken, is believed to have belonged after his death to a Mr. Linley, but in whose possession it is now has not been ascertained'.

After reading the above extracts, which are not without their errors, (for example, Miller died after Linley, and not before) it seems probable that Hardy was commissioned by Bland to paint a series of portraits of musicians, including Miller, with a view to their being engraved for publication. On acquiring the business and the engravings in 1797, it is possible that Linley found he had the engraving of his former master.

The portrait presented by Dr. Miller to the St. George's Lodge, Doncaster (No. 242) of Free and Accepted Masons was almost certainly an engraving from the Hardy portrait. The Lodge's records for December 9th 1795 tell of the R.W. Master (Dr. Miller) having presented a portrait of himself *finely engraved,* and later refer to it as a *print* or portrait. This also has long since disappeared.

On October 2nd 1807 a few weeks after the death of his father, Isaac Brailsford was appointed Organist of Doncaster at a yearly salary of fifty guineas (£52.50p). (C.R.D. Vol. 4, p. 274). He came to live at 'Church Hill', his father's old home, and in the 'Gazette' of October 9th offered his services as a teacher of singing, the pianoforte and violin. It was at this house that most of his family of six sons and five daughters were born, and for many years his wife Nancy kept a boarding school there. A notice in the 'Gazette' of March 21st 1817 stated that Mrs. Brailsford would open a school for young ladies at 'Church Hill' in the autumn of that year. We read in the same paper on July 19th 1833 that she had removed the school to more commodious premises in Hallgate, and this house became the family home as well, for a concert notice of March 6th 1835, gave Isaac's address as Hallgate too (ibid). Only a month later Mrs. Brailsford denied the rumour, through the same columns, that her school was closing and that she was leaving the town. She explained that she was transferring the school to her daughter Lois, but would continue to advise and assist. Also in the same year, 1835, Isaac resigned his post as organist, due to some disagreement with the church officials. Hatfield writes of 'his career being somewhat dimmed by a too free indulgence in social pleasures' ('Historical Notices', Vol. 1, p. 404). He was succeeded at St. George's by Mr. Jeremiah Rogers, and we hear no more of Isaac as organist until 1839 when he was appointed to the organ of Priory Place Wesleyan Methodist Chapel in Doncaster. At the opening of a new organ there in that year the three recitalists were Jeremiah Rogers, Isaac Brailsford, and Isaac's son Edward, who was organist of Christ Church, Doncaster (1833-40) and later became a priest. Isaac died on July 29th 1842 at his home in Cartwright Street (named after the inventor) and the memorial slab in the churchyard gave his age as 64. His wife died at the same address in 1844. Some information concerning the Brailsfords will be found in Appendix Four, but one son must be mentioned here, not because of a distinguished career, but because of his name. George Smart Brailsford was named after George Smart, his father's fellow chorister at His Majesty's Chapel Royal, who later became Sir George Smart. (See page 54). It will perhaps be recalled that Sir George's father, George Smart, Senior, was a member with Dr. Miller of the small deputation that waited on Lord Sydney in 1789 with the address of the New Musical Fund to His Majesty, on the occasion of his happy recovery.

Of Isaac's brother, Edward, mercer of Doncaster, whom we must not confuse with his son of the same name, the little that is known is given in the same Appendix.

It is fitting that we close this chapter by bringing the story of 'Church Hill' up to date, and telling also of the Miller Memorial Service at St. George's in 1937, which was attended by some of his descendants. William Edward, after ministering in many Wesleyan Methodist Circuits from 1799 onwards, settled as a supernumerary minister in Sheffield and died there on November 12th 1839. His wife Mary had died in 1833. After his death, his estate, including 'Church Hill', passed to his surviving children, one son and five daughters. (See Appendix Three). The Brailsfords had left the house in 1833 or soon afterwards, for the Water Rate book for 1835 described it as 'empty'. It is not known who occupied it next, but by 1846, John Allison, formerly of Rotherham, was living there. He had been appointed by the Corporation of Doncaster as Master of the English School in 1811. (C.R.D. Vol. 4, p. 276). This was a Corporation Free School for the sons of poorer freemen, and when it closed in 1822 (C.R.D. Vol. 4, p. 291), Allison started his own school, first in St. Sepulchre Gate and later in Priory Place. ('Gazette', July 15th 1825 and January 17th 1845). When he died at 'Church Hill' in 1859 his son, John Allison, Junior, became tenant and continued the school. In his 'Historical Notices of Doncaster' (Vol. 1, p. 381), Hatfield refers to the residence of Dr. Miller being tenanted by John Allison, schoolmaster, in 1866. Two years later 'Church Hill', Miller's Yard and property in Church Street, was sold by William Edward's surviving trustee for £625, on behalf of the five remaining children, all daughters. The purchaser was Benjamin James Eyre, who had married Julia, William Edward's fifth and youngest daughter (Sheffield City Library Baxter Papers. 62123). When this Benjamin James Eyre, merchant and manufacturer, of Rockingham Street, Sheffield died on September 5th 1878, the property became vested in his widow, and John Allison remained tenant of 'Church Hill' until his death in 1882. A Sale of school and household furniture, together with four hundred volumes, took place on the premises in 1883. ('Gazette', December 21st). In the same month the house was leased to John Henry Scales, bootmaker, for seven years with an option to purchase for £240. On the termination of this lease the bootmaker bought, not only 'Church Hill' with its outbuildings, yard and garden, but the entire property including Miller's Yard with its five dwellings, and numbers one to four Church Street. For this he paid

ST. GEORGE'S CHURCH FROM THE NORTH-EAST.
In the right foreground is Miller's house, 'Church Hill', with Miller's Yard under partial demolition in the centre of the picture. (From an etching by W. K. Mortlock, 1936).

£740 (Doncaster Archives, Envelope J9.19). In 1908, 'Church Hill' only, was purchased by the Rev. F. G. Sandford, Vicar of Doncaster, and Edward Newsum, accountant and churchwarden, this acquisition being announced during the Jubilee Commemoration of the rebuilding of the Parish Church. It was to be used as a hostel for the assistant clergy, a function which it still serves in addition to housing parish meeting rooms and offices. After the death of John Henry Scales (October 16th 1919) the Miller's Yard and Church Street property was sold to James Crawford, cattle dealer, who sold it to the Doncaster Corporation in March 1925. It was intended to be the site for a new Fire Station but this project never materialized, and subsequently the property was demolished. In 1966, when the Corporation required a part of the churchyard for construction of the inner ring road, an exchange was made. The sites formerly occupied by Miller's Yard and numbers one to four Church Street were again united with 'Church Hill', the property being vested in the Sheffield Diocesan Trust and Board of Finance. (Doncaster Archives. Envelope J9.19).

On the morning of Sunday, October 24th 1937 a large congregation assembled in the Parish Church at Doncaster for the Miller Memorial Service. Archdeacon Richard Brook, Rector of Rugby, formerly Vicar of Doncaster, and later to become Bishop of St. Edmundsbury and Ipswich, preached the sermon, his text being 'Let us now praise famous men - such as found out musical tunes and recited verses in writing'. As may be expected, one of the chosen hymns was 'When I survey the wond'rous Cross', to the tune 'Rockingham', and the Nunc Dimittis from Miller's Service in C was also sung. (See p.53). During the service a tablet, placed on the wall of the north transept near the organ, was unveiled by Mrs. Bramwell of Baughurst, near Basingstoke, the Doctor's great, great, granddaughter, whom we met briefly in Chapter Twelve. It bore the inscription -

'In memory of Edward Miller, Mus. Doc., and in gratitude for the tune 'Rockingham' which he composed while organist of this church, 1757-1807. This tablet is placed here by some who love the tune'.

Other descendants present were Mrs. Mason MacFarlane of Angus, a cousin of Mrs. Bramwell; Major T. H. Denman of Southampton; Mrs. Stenhouse of Bournemouth and Mrs. Lea of Chesham Bois. Letters of apology were received from two of Mrs. Bramwell's brothers, Sir Edward Farquhar Buzzard, Bart., K.C.V.O., Physician-in-Ordinary to His Majesty, and Brigadier-General Frank Anstie Buzzard. All the above were descendants of Joseph Wass, a lead merchant and smelter of Matlock, and his wife Ann, who was William Edward Miller's second daughter. (See Appendix Three). Joseph and Ann Wass had two daughters, Blanche Miller Wass and Isabel Wass. The former married

Francis Edmund Anstie and from them the Mason MacFarlanes were descended. Isabel married Thomas Buzzard and they were the parents of Sir Farquhar and Brigadier-General Frank Buzzard and of Mrs. Bramwell. Sir Farquhar's eldest son was christened Anthony Wass Buzzard, (later Sir Anthony Wass Buzzard, C.B., D.S.O., O.B.E., the second baronet), and another son was Edward Miller Buzzard.

During his sermon Archdeacon Brook told how the tablet came to be erected. The Rev. A. G. E. Gibson of Hallgate Congregational Church, Doncaster, was attending an assembly of Congregational Churches in London at which there were representatives of Christian churches from many parts of the world. During an interval he asked if those who sang the tune 'Rockingham' in their own churches, to the words of Isaac Watts, or a translation of them, would each contribute a shilling (5p) towards the cost of erecting a memorial to Dr. Miller in Doncaster Parish Church. Among those who subscribed that day were representatives from churches in Africa, Australia, North and South America, China, Egypt and Ceylon. When the Rev. Mr. Gibson left Doncaster in 1931 he handed over the money to the Vicar, Canon Brook, who decided to postpone the erection of the memorial until the cleaning and renovating of the organ was completed. It seems unfortunate that, with the passing of more than six years from the inception of this project to its completion, a little time was not devoted by those primarily concerned to checking the accuracy of their information. Miller did not compose 'Rockingham' and never claimed to have done so. Neither was he appointed organist in 1757. The 'Gazette' of October 21st, published just before the service, drew attention to both these errors, and as already stated in Chapter Two, the 'Calendar of the Records of Doncaster' (C.R.D. Vol. 4, p. 227), recorded the appointment of Edward Miller on August 19th 1756.

The most famous of the Miller descendants neither attended the service nor sent an apology for absence. He did not, in fact, know anything about it.

On the 30th of December 1937, this paragraph, written by the Editor, appeared in the 'Doncaster Gazette' -

'There has been a good deal about our old Doncaster organist and historian, Dr. Edward Miller, in these notes lately, and I hope my readers will not deem the topic threadbare. I have recently discovered something about the old fellow, however, which so far has not appeared in print - I think not, at any rate. If my information is correct (and up to the present I have not been able to obtain absolute confirmation of it) the various descendants of this eighteenth century musician include a distinguished American author whose name is as well-known in this country as in the land of his birth.'

In 1827 William Edward's third daughter, Mary, married Charles Hall of Sheffield. (See Appendix Three.) They emigrated to America where Charles is known to have had a hardware business in Chicago. It is possible that he represented a firm of Sheffield cutlers, for large quantities of cutlery were exported to North America in the nineteenth century, and it was the practice of some Sheffield firms to have representatives and warehouses overseas. The son of Charles and Mary Hall, Ernest Miller Hall, was born before his parents emigrated, and he also became a hardware dealer in Chicago. He married Caroline Hancock and they had a daughter, Grace Ernestine Hall. The latter married a Chicago physician, Clarence Edmunds Hemingway, and one of their children was Ernest Miller Hemingway, soldier of fortune, big game hunter, deep sea fisherman and writer. ('A Farewell to Arms', 1929; 'For Whom the Bell Tolls', 1940; 'The Old Man and the Sea', 1952, etc).

Thus Dr. Miller was Ernest Hemingway's great, great, great, grandfather!

Chapter Fifteen

Though there are still hymn-lovers who associate Edward Miller with the tune 'Rockingham', and local historians, particularly in and around South Yorkshire, who are familiar with his 'History of Doncaster', his name is quite unknown to most people today - and yet, two hundred years ago, before 'Rockingham' was arranged or the 'History' written, and in spite of living in the provinces, away from the centre of artistic activity, he was considered a father-figure in English music.

In the final chapter let us briefly examine the reasons for his success, and for regarding him as a musician worthy of remembrance.

His work over a long period for fellow musicians and for the Church made him widely known in all walks of life throughout the land. The nobility, gentry, and leading figures in the country's musical life became aware of him when he addresssd letters to them on behalf of provincial musicians, just before the Handel Commemoration of 1784 (See p. 50). The rules of the long established Music Fund of the Society of Musicians did not seem to preclude provincials from becoming members and enjoying the benefits, but they must have been prevented in some way, for Miller's statement that - 'at present, Professors residing in the country are excluded from receiving any benefit from that fund' - far from being contradicted led directly to the establishment of the New Musical Fund under the patronage of His Majesty. Money for this new society had to come chiefly from donations and concert receipts, and Edward's participation as conductor at important London concerts arranged for this purpose, made him known personally to a large number of concert-goers in the capital, while at the same time earning for him the gratitude of fellow country-musicians. In 1792, when he published a pamphlet with the title of, 'A letter to the "Country Spectator" in reply to the Author of his Ninth Number', he again spoke out for provincial music and musicians. An article on December 4th 1792 in the 'Country Spectator', a six-page weekly published in Gainsborough, spoke in contemptuous terms of musical professors and performances outside the capital. Edward's spirited reply was refused publication by the Editor, whereupon he had it printed privately by William Miller of number five, Old Bond Street, and W. Sheardown of Doncaster.

His work for the reformation of music in the Established Church made him known to a much larger and quite different body of people - to the priesthood rather than the nobility, to the musicians of the Church rather than those of stage and concert-hall, and to congregations throughout the land. The reforms advocated by the small group of pioneers, of which he was one, led to the abolition of the Clerk as an influence in the music of the Church, the greater involvement of congregations in the services, and the gradual development of the nineteenth-century church choir of men and boys, generally seated in choir-stalls in the chancel.

Important though the above activities for the Church and fellow musicians were, Edward was first and foremost a teacher, with a lasting desire to help the young music-maker. One of his earliest publications, 'Short Airs or Minuets', for the German Flute and Harpsichord, written when he was a youth, was addressed to 'young practitioners', and half a century later, similar words appeared in his last book, 'A Musical Primer', for young beginners. We may know but little of his work as a teacher of private pupils, or as a music-master in schools for young ladies and gentlemen, but there is no doubt that his books of instruction for students of the German Flute, the Harpsichord and Pianoforte, the Organ and Musical Composition, were outstanding examples of their kind two centuries ago, and as a result, most successful publications. They have the simplicity and 'gradualness' of approach so essential to the beginner, with well thought-out teaching methods, the fruit of his long experience. We see him also as a pioneer and innovator. His 'Six Solos for a German Flute' (Op. 1, 1761), though not primarily a book of instruction, has a full page of help for the young, in which 'double tongueing' was mentioned apparently for the first time in the English language. These 'Six Solos', or sonatas, which form Miller's Op. 1, especially the first and last, compare favourably with the flute sonatas of Handel (Op. 1) and Stanley (Op. 1 and 2), and modern performers on the Baroque Flute are delighted to 'discover' them. It was not until almost forty years later, during which time the one-keyed German Flute had acquired more keys, and a four-keyed version had gradually been succeeded by the six-keyed instrument, that Miller wrote 'The New Flute Instructor' (1800), a simple but thorough and up-to-date method for young beginners.

In the 'Institutes of Music, or Easy Instruction for the Harpsichord' (Op. 4), we see Edward as a pioneer of the school music text book, perhaps the first music book for class use to appear in this country. In spite of costing half a guinea (52½p), more than a week's wage for many people at that time, it was most successful, at least twenty-five editions being produced. His idea of devising a book from which a whole class could study at the same time, each at his or her own speed, while the master helped individual members in turn, is still a feature of class teaching today, and the Question and Answer method of learning has also been popular from that time. He was not quite correct in thinking that the method was a new one, however, for Thomas Morley's 'Plaine and Easie Introduction to Practicall Musicke' (1597) was also written in dialogue form.

'Elements of Thorough Bass and Composition' (Op. 5), for the student of harmony and composition, must also have been a pioneer work, being described by a writer in the 'York Courant' (Sept. 21st 1807) as the first of its kind. At least six editions were printed. Three of the later works, (Op. 7, 8, and 'A Musical Primer'), were for further study when the 'Institutes' had been completed, while Op. 9, 'Sixteen Easy Voluntaries for the Organ', had a dual purpose, for in addition to providing practice material, being originally written by the Doctor for one of his pupils, thirteen of the two-movement pieces were intended as voluntaries for use during and after services, and the remaining three for special occasions.

In the two larger works - 'Psalms of David' and 'History of Doncaster' - we again see the teacher and pioneer. The former was not just one more collection of metrical psalms and tunes, but a carefully thought-out book aimed at achieving the maximum congregational participation in the music of the services. The latter reveals the author, with his lively interest in the surroundings, his wide knowledge of ancient and modern scholarship relating to the area, and his long literary experience, as one most capable of becoming Doncaster's first historian.

Finally we must consider Edward Miller, not as a teacher but as a composer. His surviving 'non-teaching' compositions are not numerous, consisting of Op. 1 and 2, a little church music, three books of songs and some songs in sheet-music form. The 'Six Sonatas for the Harpsichord' (Op. 2) is a disappointing and rather uninspired work and something of an anti-climax after the flute sonatas of Op.1. The second of the harpsichord sonatas (Allegro and Minuet in F Major) is generally regarded as the most successful.

His songs, however, are always of interest and worthy of revival. They show him to have been well aware of the musical development which took place during his long career. The first two of his song-books - 'A Collection of New English Songs and a Cantata', and 'Elegies, Songs and an Ode' (Op. 3) have a freshness and tunefulness reminiscent of Dr. Thomas Arne. His third collection - 'Twelve Canzonets' (Op. 10), by contrast, seems to show the influence of Haydn, being similar in mood and content to the great composer's 'Twelve English Canzonets', which are amongst the finest of Haydn's songs.

A complete list of Miller's works will be found in Appendix Five, while Appendix Seven gives details of those performed in recent years in and around Doncaster.

The family of THOMAS MILLER + * and ELIZABETH —

1.	ELIZABETH	bp - 16.11.1729	
2.	THOMAS**	bp - 5. 9.1731	
3.	SARAH	bp - 23.12.1733	Second wife of Dr. Norford
4.	EDWARD	b - 30.10.1735	d - 12.9.1807
		bp - 30.11.1735	Organist of Doncaster
		See APPENDIX TWO	
5.	MARY	bp - 26.10.1740	
6.	JANE	bp - 18. 1.1742-3	
7.	LOUISE (LOIS?)	bp - 21. 9.1746	

+ The registers of St. Peter Mancroft Church, Norwich also have the following -

ELIZABETH MILLER bd 2.5.1756, aged 48

THOMAS MILLER, paviour and widower,
married TABITHA BEVIS - 12.3.1761

THOMAS MILLER bd - 12.9.1764, aged 65

Most probably these refer to the parents above.

* Thomas Miller had a brother JOHN, also a paviour.

No other brothers or sisters have been traced.

** Thomas Miller, the eldest son, became a bookseller at Bungay.
He had a son, WILLIAM RICHARD BECKFORD MILLER (1769-1844)
See APPENDIX TWO

b - born;   bc - born approx;   bp - baptized;   m - married;   d - died;   bd - buried.

APPENDIX TWO

The family of EDWARD MILLER + * and ELIZABETH LEE**
(married 15.2.1763)

1.	THOMAS	bp - 28.12.1763	bd - 1. 4.1764
2.	ELIZABETH	bp - 26.12.1764	d - 11.12.1786, aged 22 bd - 15.12.1786
3.	WILLIAM EDWARD	b - 1. 6.1766 bp - 10. 7.1766	d - 12.11.1839, aged 73 See APPENDIX THREE
4.	SARAH	bp - 27.10.1767	bd - 22. 3.1768
5.	MARY	bp - 26. 1.1769 m - her cousin WILLIAM RICHARD BECKFORD MILLER 31.7.1790	d - 6. 6.1791, aged 22 See APPENDIX ONE
6.	THOMAS	bp - 26. 1.1770 drowned at sea, 1785, aged 15	
7.	DIANA	dates of birth unknown	bd - 29. 6.1773 ⎫
8.	ALICE	may have been twins	bd - 9. 1.1774 ⎭
9.	LOIS	bp - 21. 2.1772	d - 7. 7.1792, aged 20 bd - 11. 7.1792
10.	JANE	bp - 18. 8.1773	probably d. in infancy

+ For Edward's issue by Elizabeth Brailsford - See APPENDIX FOUR

* Edward married secondly, MARGARET EDWARDS 29.12.1796
No issue. Margaret died 28.5.1838

** Elizabeth Lee, b. Doncaster - 8.8.1745, d - 14.8.1773, aged 28

The family of WILLIAM EDWARD MILLER and MARY DUNHILL*
(married 13.12.1792)

1.	ELIZABETH LOIS	bc - 1794 m - JOHN ALSOP	living in 1868
2.	ANN	bc - 1796 m - JOSEPH WASS, 8.9.1826	d - 6.9.1882
3.	MARY	bc - 1798 m - CHAS HALL, 1827	living in 1869 (U.S.A.)
4.	LOUISA	bc - 1800 m - JOHN WATHEY, 1850	d - 17.3.1879
5.	JULIA	bc - 1801 m - BENJAMIN J. EYRE, 1840	living in 1890
6.	THOMAS	bc - 1803 at school, 1812-18	d - before 1839
7.	WILLIAM EDWARD	bc - 1803 at school, 1812-18	d - 22.7.1856 in S. America (Mineowner)
8.	JOSEPH	bc - 1806 at school, 1817-20	d - before 1839
9.	CHARLES WESLEY	bc - 1810 at school, 1819-25	d - 25.12.1831 in Chile

All four boys were on the registers of Kingswood and Woodhouse Grove Schools.

* Mary Dunhill, daughter of Alderman Dunhill of Doncaster, bp - 21.8.1769,
d - 30.3.1833, aged 63

The family of ISAAC BRAILSFORD* + and NANCY WILLSON**
(married 26. 1. 1802)

1.	WILLSON	bp - 8. 6.1803 Methodist Minister	d - 3.3.1882, aged 78
2.	MARY ELIZABETH	bp - 10. 4.1806	d - 30.7.1865 at Bradford
3.	EDWARD	bp - 28.12.1807 Organist, Ch.Ch., Doncaster, 1833-40. Later in Holy Orders	
4.	HODGSON	b - 18. 3.1809 bp - 22. 5.1809	d - 10.3.1874 Graduate Tr. College Dublin Rector, D.D.
5.	LOIS	bp - 23.11.1810	
6.	ISAAC	bp - 6. 9.1812 m - 1830	d - 23.11.1872
7.	EMMA	b - 20.10.1813 bp - 26. 6.1814	m - 1835 and 1858
8.	THOMAS RICHARD	bp - 6. 3.1816 Of Trinity College, Dublin	d - September, 1853
9.	GEORGE SMART	b - 3. 3.1818 bp - 5. 7.1820	d - 19.6.1841, aged 23
10.	AGNES	b - 2. 2.1820 bp - 5. 7.1820	m - 1848
11.	ELIZA JANE	b - 30. 5.1822 bp - 18. 8.1826	d - 23.6.1849, at Hull

* Isaac Brailsford b - 1777 or 1778. d - 29.7.1842, aged 64
  Organist Bradford and Doncaster

** Nancy Willson, daughter of Isaac Willson of Bradford, bp - 25.12.1783,
  d - 17.2.1844, aged 60

+ Isaac's brother, EDWARD bp - 1.8.1785, d - 8.5.1822, aged 36; m -RICHMOND
  DIXON, daughter of James Dixon, farmer of Upton, at Badsworth in 1815. They had
  a son, CHARLES JAMES BRAILSFORD, who married ELIZABETH FENTON of
  Cheadle in October, 1838. Charles James died - 9.12.1841, aged 25

CATALOGUE OF WORKS

* c 1754   A Collection of New English Songs and a Cantata.

c 1754   Short Airs or Minuets composed for the use of young practitioners on the German Flute and Harpsichord.

1761   Op. 1. Six Solos for a German Flute with a thorough bass for the Harpsichord or Violoncello.

c 1768   Op. 2. Six Sonatas for the Harpsichord, with an accompaniment to three of them for a Violin or German Flute.

* c 1770   Op. 3. Elegies, Songs, and an Ode of Mr. Pope's, with Instrumental parts.

1782   (Pamphlet) The Tears of Yorkshire for the Loss of the Most Noble, the Marquis of Rockingham.

1783   Op. 4. Institutes of Music, or Easy Instruction for the Harpsichord.

1784   (Pamphlet) Letters in behalf of Professors of Music residing in the Country.

1787   Op. 5. Elements of Thorough Bass and Composition.

1789   Op. 6. An Anthem and Hymn, with Instrumental parts.

1789   Book One - Six Sonatas from Corelli, Op. 1 arranged for the Organ, and Six from Op. 2 arranged for Harpsichord or Pianoforte.
Book Two - Six Sonatas from Corelli, Op. 3 and Six from Op. 4 arranged similarly.

1790   The Psalms of David, for the Use of Parish Churches.

1791   (Pamphlet) Thoughts on the present performance of Psalmody in the Established Church of England.

1791   Op. 7. Twenty-four Exercises in all the Major and Minor Keys.

1791   Op. 8. Twelve Progressive Lessons for the Piano Forte or Harpsichord, with an Accompaniment for the Violin or Flute.

1792   (Pamphlet) A Letter to the 'Country Spectator'.

1797   Op. 9. Sixteen Easy Voluntaries for the Organ.

* c 1799   Op. 10. Twelve Canzonets for the Voice and Pianoforte.

1800   The New Flute Instructor.

1800   Music to Dr. Watts's Psalms and Hymns, with Appendix. Volume One.

1804   The History and Antiquities of Doncaster and its Vicinity.

1805   Music to Dr. Watts's Psalms and Hymns, with Appendix. Volume Two.

1805   An Anthem performed on a Commencement at St. Mary's Church, Cambridge, and a Hymn.

1807   A Musical Primer.

?   Te Deum, Jubilate, Magnificat and Nunc Dimittis in C.

Songs in Sheet Music Form, definitely published —

1788   Fair Sophia. Words by Hon. Horace Walpole.

1788   Serious Epigram. Words by Sir William Jones.

1790   Ye Britons Bold.

1790   I'm monarch of all I survey.

1790   The afflicted African.

c 1794   Britons ever shall be free. Words by the Duke of Leeds.

c 1795   The Negro Boy.

c 1799   I'll live no more single (Glee) - also known as 'Variety'.
I prithee send me back my heart - This song with words by Sir John Suckling, is one of the four songs by Miller, with accompaniment by C. Armstrong Gibbs, published in 1937. Of the other three, one came from his 'Elegies' (To Althea from Prison) and the other two, (The Happy Pair and The Despairing Shepherd) from his first publication, 'A Collection of New English Songs and a Cantata'.

* See page 139.

CATALOGUE OF WORKS (Continued)

Songs performed, but most probably never published —

Address to Robin Redbreast. Words by Peter Pindar. (Sung by Mrs. Ilife, accompanied on a small flute by Mr. Darcy at Doncaster Theatre, 1788).
Ode and Song written in honour of H.R.H. the Prince of Wales on his visit to Wentworth House, 1789.
Bishop Blaize. Words by Matthew Charlton, 1792.
The Queen of France. Her lamentation before her execution. 1793.
War and Justice. 1794.
Song for Free Masons. 1797.
The Little French Emigrée. Words by Mrs. McGeorge. 1798.
The Soldier's Adieu. 1799 - said to be a vocal version of a March by Miller for the Fifth West Yorkshire Militia.

* Titles of the pieces in his three song books —

c 1754 'A Collection of New English Songs and a Cantata' —

Nancy. Words by Mr. Robinson.	The Second Ode of Anacreon.
The Happy Pair. Words by Mr. Pilkington (Part for German Flute).	Advice to the Ladies. Strephon and Chloe.
The Despairing Shepherd. Words by Sir Carr Scroope.	Cantata. Words by Mr. Robinson, Part for the Violin.

c 1770 'Elegies, Songs and an Ode of Mr. Pope's'. Op. 3—
    The Wand'ring Nymph. Words from the Greek.
    A Pastoral Elegy.
    Song. 'Wrote by Colonel Lovelace in Prison'.
    The Sweet Neglect. Words by Ben Jonson.
    Margaret's Ghost.
    Elegy on the Death of Mr. Handel.
    Ode. Words by Mr. Pope.

c 1799 'Twelve Canzonets for the Voice and Pianoforte'. Op. 10—
    When thy beauty appears. Words by Dean Parnell.
    Verses written by Mary, Queen of Scots, in sailing from Calais to Dover, 1560.
    Poor Little Rosalie.
    An Address to Sleep.
    The Primrose.
    Sweet maid, remember me.
    Cynthia. Words by Peter Pindar.
    If a tender maid you love.
    Amanda.
    Fair Ann was the pride of the West.
    Glistening Dewdrops.
    Come, come, for you've promised.

All the above songs are written for the Soprano voice. Occasionally a second part for the Bass is added, as in the short Cantata which ends the first book, and a few songs have parts for Violin, Flute or Guitar.

A very comprehensive, though not a complete collection of the above works, may be seen in the Music Library of the British Library, and there is another in the University

Library, Cambridge. His works are well represented in the Reference Library at Doncaster, though some of them are only photostatic copies. Seemingly scarce works can be found elsewhere - the 'Sixteen Easy Voluntaries for the Organ' (Op. 9) in the Bodleian Library, Oxford; his two songs from the 'Lady's Musical Magazine' of November 1788 in the Rowe Music Library, King's College, Cambridge; a subscription copy of the music edition to Dr. Watts's 'Psalms and Hymns, with Appendix' in the Henry Watson Music Library, Manchester; and 'Letters on behalf of Professors of Music residing in the Country' in the Leeds City Library, where there is also a copy of Op. 4, 'Institutes of Music', and Op. 9, 'Sixteen Easy Voluntaries for the Organ'.

* * * * *

APPENDIX SIX

HARRIS'S ORGAN, 1739 - 40

(from the 'History and Description of St. George's Church at Doncaster' by the Rev. J. E. Jackson, M.A.)

SPECIFICATION

GREAT ORGAN	number of pipes		CHOIR ORGAN	number of pipes
1. Open Diapason, of metal (front)	52		1. Stopped Diapason	52
2. Open Diapason (back)	52		2. Flute	52
3. Stopped Diapason	52		3. Fifteenth	52
4. Principal, of metal	52		4. Bassoon	52
5. Twelfth, ditto	52		5. Vox humana. (This does	52
6. Fifteenth, ditto	52		not appear in the	260
7. Tierce, ditto	52		original contract, but	
8. Sesquialtra of 5 ranks	260		there is no doubt that	
9. Cornet of 5 ranks, mounted (middle C to D)	135		it was added at the time)	
10. Trumpet (front)	52		ECHO OR SWELL ORGAN	
11. Trumpet (back)	52		1. Open Diapason	27
12. Clarion	52		2. Stopped Diapason	27
	915		3. Principal	27
			4. Cornet of 3 ranks	81
			5. Trumpet	27
			6. Hautboy	27

Making altogether 23 stops, with 1391 pipes. The compass of the Great and Choir Organs was from GG to D; but it had what are called 'Short Octaves'. The compass of the Swell Organ was from middle C up to D. The Echo Organ was placed under the sound-boards of the Great Organ. The peculiarity of this Organ consisted in having in the Great Organ two trumpets and a clarion throughout the whole compass.

In 1758 it was repaired and tuned by John Snetzler.

In 1802, Dr. Miller being organist, Mr. Donaldson of York substituted a Dulciana in the place of the Fifteenth in the Choir Organ, and carried the Swell Organ, at that time of very limited compass, down from middle C to fiddle G.

SOME SOUTH YORKSHIRE CONCERT PERFORMANCES OF DR. MILLER'S WORKS

Doncaster Museum and Art Gallery

October 14th 1970	'Flute Sonata in C' (Op. 1. No. 1) edited for oboe by Roger Bullivant - Thelma Marion (oboe), Roger Bullivant (harpsichord) and Eric Stuart ('cello).
March 2nd 1971	'Variety', a glee for three voices - The Arcadian Singers.
January 26th 1972	'Harpsichord Sonata in F' (Op. 2. No. 2) Magnus Black (piano).
March 21st 1973	Song, 'The Negro Boy' - Leslie Gronow (tenor) and Paul Herrington (piano).
February 5th 1977	'Flute Sonata in D' (Op. 1. No. 6) Songs, 'A Pastoral Elegy', 'The Happy Pair' and 'An Address to Sleep' (with a part for the flute). The glee 'Variety' and hymn-tune 'Tunbridge' - Alistair Roberts (modern flute), Ruth Williams (soprano), The Doncaster Choral Guild and David Hainsworth (piano).
July 19th 1977	'Harpsichord Sonata in F' (Op. 2. No. 2) - Gerald Gifford (harpsichord).
April 18th 1979	Songs, 'The Wand'ring Nymph' and 'The Despairing Shepherd' - Angela Hartley (mezzo-soprano) and Rachel Richardson (piano).

Doncaster Parish Church

October 11th 1966	'Magnificat and Nunc Dimittis in C'.
September 26th 1970	'Organ Sonata in F', arranged from Corelli's Trio Sonata (Op. 1. No. 1)
October 21st 1970	'Organ Sonata in D', arranged from Corelli's Trio Sonata (Op. 2. No. 1)
November 20th 1971	'Organ Sonata in D Min.', arranged from Corelli's Trio Sonata (Op. 1. No. 11)
November 25th 1972	'Sixteen Easy Voluntaries for the Organ' (Op. 9 numbers 1, 2, 3, 5, 7 and 9) - The Parish Church Choir, with Magnus Black (organist).

High Melton Hall (Doncaster College of Education)

June 30th 1971	'Flute Sonata in C' (Op. 1. No. 1) - Robert Hunter (modern flute) and Magnus Black (piano).

Danum Grammar School, Doncaster

November 10th 1977	'Flute Sonata in D' (Op. 1. No.6) - Nicholas McGegan (baroque flute) and Peter Seymour (harpsichord).

Cusworth Hall

July 14th 1978	'Flute Sonatas in C and D' (Op. 1. No's. 1 and 6) 'Harpsichord Sonata in F' (Op. 2. No. 2) Songs, 'By Colonel Lovelace in Prison' and 'A Pastoral Elegy' - Judith Simmons (mezzo-soprano), Utako Ikeda (baroque flute) and Paul Nicholson (harpsichord).

DONCASTER
TO BE SOLD BY AUCTION

At the House of the late Dr. Miller, in Doncaster, on
Thursday the 12th Day of November 1807.

All the HOUSEHOLD GOODS and FURNITURE, late
belonging to the said DR. MILLER, deceased,
consisting of Mahogany and other Bedsteads, Feather
Beds, and Bedding, Mahogany and other Chairs,
Tables and Chests of Drawers, Pier and Swing
Looking Glasses, a neat Mahogany Side board Table
(new), a good Harpsichord, Two old Ditto, Piano
Forte, and other Musical Instruments, several good
Prints, and particularly Two Sets of Hogarth's Prints
of the Rake's and Harlot's Progress, very scarce,
Glass, China, and Earthen ware, Kitchen Utensils,
Brewing Vessels, and various other Articles.

The Sale to begin at Ten o'Clock in the Forenoon.

From the 'Doncaster, Nottingham and Lincoln Gazette'.
Nov. 6th 1807.